THE BIG BOOK OF
THAI CURRIES

THE BIG BOOK OF
THAI CURRIES

VATCHARIN BHUMICHITR

Photography by **Martin Brigdale**
and **Somchai Phongphaisarnkit**

Kyle Books

For my sister

Published in 2007 by Kyle Books, an imprint of
Kyle Cathie Limited
www.kylecathie.com

Distributed by National Book Network
4501 Forbes Blvd., Suite 200
Lanham, MD 20706
Phone: (301) 459 3366 Fax: (301) 429 5746

10 9 8 7 6 5 4 3 2 1

ISBN 978-1-904920-77-9

Project editor **Jennifer Wheatley**
Designer **Fran Rawlinson**
Photographer **Martin Brigdale** and **Somchai Phongphaisarnkit**
Food styling **Annie Rigg** (apart from pages 97, 116, 123, 132, 135, 149, 169; **Linda Tubby**)
Styling **Helen Trent**
Copy editor **Stephanie Evans** and **Vanessa Kendell**
Americanizer **Delora Jones**
Production **Sha Huxtable** and **Alice Holloway**

Vatcharin Bhumichitr is hereby identified as the author of this work in accordance with
Section 77 of the Copyright, Designs and Patents Act 1988.

Library of Congress Control Number: 2007931463

Printed in China

CONTENTS

INTRODUCTION

"KIN KHAO LUA LANG!"

This is the traditional greeting you will hear all over Thailand. Unlike Western greetings, it doesn't mean "how are you?" or "hello." It means "have you eaten yet?". This shows just how central food is to the Thai way of life. If the reply is "no," the greeting will often be followed by an invitation to eat. And for a group of Thais sitting down to a meal, the first question is invariably "kin gaeng arai dee?" or "what curry shall we eat?". The type of curry (green, red, yellow, etc.) and the kind of meat or fish to go in it are discussed first. Only when this is decided will the conversation turn to other elements of the meal—the stir-fries or steamed dishes and their respective ingredients.

curries and thai cooking

I always feel lucky to have been born in Thailand. The country is very fertile, irrigated as it is by the great Chao Phraya and other rivers. Thailand is largely an agricultural society, growing rice, fruit, and vegetables, and raising animals. The Gulf of Thailand is teeming with fish, the climate is good and most foods grow very easily here. If you stay in the countryside, you quickly become aware that nearly all you need to survive grows around you. In the villages, a strong culture of sharing resources was once common; one household would slaughter an animal and it would be shared among everyone in the village.

Rice farmers in Thailand are the backbone of Thai agriculture and their crop is the lifeblood of Thailand. Glutinous or "sticky" rice is popular in the north and northeast, but in the rest of the country the long-grain variety is dominant. For many years, rice was the country's main export and it still remains the staple part of the Thai diet, providing strength and energy.

To bulk up the rice and add flavor, a spicy, fairly runny, curry sauce is always served—the effect is to make you eat more rice! Traditionally, rice is eaten three times a day, and curry can be eaten at any, or all, of these meals. As you would expect, the various regions of Thailand have developed their own specialties of curry by using their locally grown herbs and spices. The curries of the country's border regions also often reflect the cuisines of adjacent nations. There is a strong Laotian influence in the northeast, a Burmese influence in the north, Malay and Muslim influences in the south, and so on. But the culinary influence of different countries goes beyond Thailand's immediate neighbors. Sri Lanka, India, and Iran have all had their inputs, but now Thai curries have developed their own individual tastes, colors, and textures.

My mother's specialty was green beef curry. In a big family like ours, she would cook a large pot of curry to feed us all. My father was always busy working or entertaining, but whenever he ate at home he would ask for green curry. I was the same; just before term ended when I was studying in London, I phoned home to ensure a curry would be ready when I arrived back in Bangkok. One of my brothers even told his future wife that his one requirement was that she learned to cook green curry just like our mother!

SERVINGS AND QUANTITIES

The recipes in this book are for four to six people, and they tell you how to make curries as authentic as you would find in Thailand. When you start making the curries, I hope you will experiment, adjusting the quantities of the ingredients to create a hotter, milder, sweeter, or more sour taste—just as cooks do in Thailand—so you develop the flavors that you prefer. The best way to learn about Thai curries is to make a big pot, invite your friends over, have a party, and enjoy yourself.

left
Different vegetables are planted in rows with irrigation channels between them. This farming technique is widely used in central Thailand, near the Chao Phraya River. Here they are planting shallots and garlic.

above right
Good quality, long-grain rice. It is always bought in bulk in Thailand!

right
Young papaya trees —these are grown from seed and can grow to about six feet in height. Here they are surrounded by coriander plants.

what is thai cooking?

Originally, Thai people lived a waterborne lifestyle, mainly in the central plains of Thailand, traveling on, and living by the rivers, growing rice and catching fish, which was cooked on a wood-fire grill or barbecue. To accompany the fish, they developed dips and sauces, which were made from locally grown herbs, spices, peppers, cucumbers, eggplants, and other vegetables, some of which were grown in the rivers, along with various types of limes and lemongrass. The vegetables were, and still are, often eaten raw. As this diet is somewhat dry, soups developed, such as the well-known *tom yam*, which was originally made with fish. At that time, the Thais shunned eating large animals, and when meat was eaten it was always chopped into small pieces. This is thought to be because of their Buddhist heritage. During the 16th century, foreigners started to appear in Thailand, introducing significant new ingredients, such as the chile. Since that time, the Thais have adopted many foreign foods, including curries from India and Persia, and noodles

from China, but they have always been adapted to suit the Thai way of eating, thereby producing a taste unique to Thailand. Food inevitably becomes individual to the place where it is being prepared and cooked, because the local ingredients always have a taste and texture different to anywhere else. Nowadays, fruit and vegetables that are associated with certain parts of the world can be bought anywhere, and so, sadly, this individuality is gradually being lost. I am glad to say, though, that it still exists in Thailand.

What does curry mean?

The word "curry" is a derivative of the Tamil word "kari." This was used in India to describe a type of dish with a strong flavor and aroma caused by the herbs and spices used in the cooking. They were often used to disguise poor-quality meat, which in the old days could be pretty tough and "high." A few Thai curries do resemble the Indian version, in which case the name *kari* is used (see Duck Curry on page 90), but the more usual term in Thailand is *gaeng pet*. This literally means "thickened spicy liquid." *Gaeng pet* has a broader application than the English word "curry" and can be used to describe any savory dish that has been thickened with a paste.

Curry paste was and still is prepared by pounding the ingredients individually in a mortar. If you walk around some residential areas in Thailand in the morning, you will hear the rhythmic pounding of mortars and pestles all around you. Each housewife produces her own characteristic beat as she grinds out the paste for that day's curry. Today, however, most people buy their curry pastes, either freshly made in the local market or prepacked from a supermarket.

Many of the ingredients in Thai curry pastes are considered healthy and even medicinal (garlic is an obvious example), but their texture or taste can make them difficult or unpleasant to eat alone. Pounding and mixing them together gets round this problem, and when the flavors are skillfully blended, ingredients that might be unpalatable on their own become part of something delicious.

left
Different ready-made curry pastes for sale.

right
An array of red, green, pale green, and yellow chilies. Bigger chiles tend to be milder and are often dried to intensify their flavor. Thai cucumbers can be seen on the far right of the picture.

Curry pastes form the basis of almost all Thai dishes —the two exceptions are soups and stir-fries. You might be surprised to find a chapter entitled "Snacks and One-Dish Meals" in a book about curries, but all these recipes use some kind of curry paste as their foundation, and that includes satay, corn cakes, and rice and noodle dishes.

The differences between a Thai and an Indian curry

The most obvious difference between Thai and Indian curries is that Thai curries are cooked with herbs and spices that are nearly always fresh, whereas Indian curries use dried ones. And while Indian curries are usually based on ghee or yogurt, Thais typically use coconut milk. The resulting textures are as subtly contrasting as cow's milk and soy milk. Another difference is that Thai curries combine vegetables with meat or fish, while in India the vegetables are often served as separate dishes.

What's special about Thai curries?

Because they are based on fresh ingredients, Thai curries are uniquely light and refreshing. They also have very distinctive colors. These are determined by the color of their ingredients, mostly the chiles and the curry pastes, hence the famous red, green, and yellow varieties.

Where does the heat in Thai curries come from?

The heat in Thai curries comes from chiles, pepper (both white and black), garlic, galangal, coriander, and onion. All these ingredients are hot in varying degrees. But while heat is a feature of many of the curries in this book, it should always be balanced by three other key tastes in Thai cuisine: sweet, sour, and salty. Sweetness is provided by ingredients such as sugar and Thai basil; sourness by tamarind and lime; and saltiness by fish sauce.

the role of curry in a thai meal

When we discuss what to eat, we first choose a type of curry (red, green, orange, jungle) and the main ingredient (beef, pork, fish, etc.). At home, after we finish dinner, we discuss what we are going to eat the following day. Once we have decided on the curry and its ingredients, we then decide on the accompanying vegetables, taking into account what is in season and so on. These will be cooked in a stir-fry. We may then choose another dish to balance the other flavors. If the curry is pork, for example, the third dish might be fish fried with garlic and chile. We also select a dessert. Early in the morning, someone will go out to the market and buy all the fresh ingredients for the evening meal. In the afternoon, we prepare the curry and the dessert, which takes about thirty minutes. The remaining dishes are cooked around 7 p.m. and ready on the table for dinner an hour later.

Curry is eaten all day

When I was at school, much like today, there was food for sale in school at lunchtime, or you could take your own lunchbox. I usually had some toast and hot chocolate, or eggs and bacon for breakfast. For lunch, I would eat curry noodles, and in the evening we would have a meal based around a curry.

In many households, particularly in the countryside, they will cook a large pot of curry early in the morning, which will be eaten throughout the day by the whole family. The children will take it to eat at school and the adults will take it out to the fields where they go to work. In the evening, it will form the basis of the evening meal, to be eaten together with a stir-fry and a soup.

When you travel on the freeways of Thailand, as in other countries, there are service stations, generally with a small selection of food outlets. In Thailand, these are normally run by local people. There will be a wide selection of precooked food, several different curries and stir-fried dishes, omelets and fried eggs. You are given a plate of boiled rice, and then you pick a spoonful or two of different dishes to be placed on top of the rice. You can choose as many as you wish, although any more than three or four toppings and the flavors can become a little confused. This will normally be eaten with a selection of raw vegetables, which, along with the condiments, will be provided for you at the table.

Street food

My family home is in the center of Bangkok, near Silom Road. When I was young, it was a quiet residential area with pleasant houses and large, leafy gardens. Now it has been redeveloped into high-rise offices and apartments. This has naturally

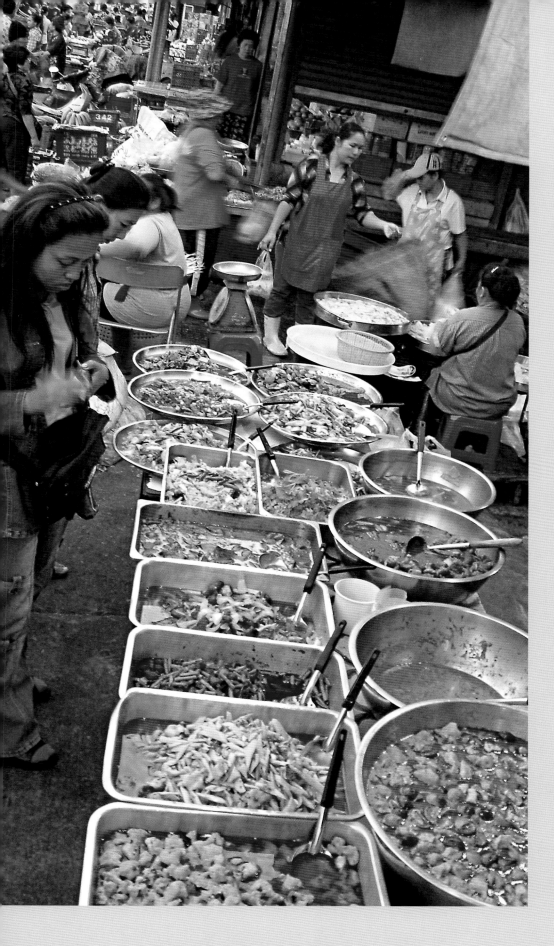

increased the number of workers and residents who need to be fed. There are now many roadside food stalls selling all manner of food. In this area, the stallholders start work at around 4 a.m., preparing breakfast: rice soup, freshly squeezed fruit juices, fresh fruit, coffee, and, of course, curry with steamed rice. Generally, the cooks on the curry stalls will begin by preparing a big pot of one type of curry, then move onto the next. Come lunchtime, they will have a selection of at least ten different curries. The food is served as quickly as any Western fast-food outlet, and small tables are set out on the sidewalk. Much is sold as take-out food to be eaten later, either at the office or at home for dinner. Lunch is generally over by 2 p.m. when the stalls are cleaned up and packed away. The cooks then go to market to buy fresh meat, vegetables, and other ingredients for the following day. Their working day is just as long as that of the office workers they feed.

far left
Smaller ingredients such as pea eggplants are often sold by the bowl rather than by weight.

left
A selection of ready-made, take-out curries.

composition of a thai curry

Why is the combination of coriander, lemongrass, and garlic so Thai?

There are three main reasons why the combination of coriander, lemongrass and garlic is so typical of Thai cooking. The first has to do with convenience. All these ingredients grow quickly and abundantly throughout Thailand and they are available all year round. Most urban households will have them growing in the garden. Lemongrass grows just like regular grass, only with more of a tendency to form clumps. Garlic and coriander are also fast growing, and the latter has the advantage of furnishing the cook with three distinct products: seeds, roots and leaves (cilantro).

The second reason for the importance of these ingredients in Thai cuisine is their contribution to a healthy diet. Unlike Westerners, Thais do not make a clear distinction between food and medicine, and all three plants are considered medicinal. Coriander is believed to enhance the appetite, improve digestion, and clear phlegm. Lemongrass is another appetite stimulant and considered to be good for headaches and fevers. Garlic, meanwhile, is thought to cleanse the blood.

Unsurprisingly, the final reason why garlic, lemongrass, and coriander are so central in Thai cooking is all about taste. All three contribute to the perfumed clarity that is so characteristic of Thai dishes, both individually and together. Garlic is used to flavor cooking oils (Thais don't like to use oils with a strong flavor of their own) and to provide an aromatic, but largely hidden, base for savory dishes. Lemongrass lends a fresh citrus taste with hints of mint and ginger. It cuts through oils and fats, giving zest to dishes that would otherwise be cloying on the palate. Coriander, as mentioned above, yields three distinct ingredients. The fibrous roots are used as a flavorful binding agent in curry pastes. The seeds are ground to produce a spice with an orange aroma, and the coriander leaves (also called cilantro) provide pungency as well as an attractive garnish.

Any Thai cook will have learned through experience the skill to balance the flavors of garlic, lemongrass, and coriander according to their own preference. As a result, the cumulative taste will vary from cook to cook and area to area. There is no such thing as the correct combination, only a personal one, which is developed over a lifetime of cooking with these three key ingredients.

left
Counterclockwise from bottom: lemongrass, kaffir lime leaves, galangal, mint, kaffir limes, krachai.

right
The whole coriander plant is used and it is sold in big bunches.

above right
Lemongrass grows very easily in Thailand. The white, tender part of the plant is the root; the leaves are chopped off and discarded.

What are the other key ingredients in Thai curries?

CHILES

These were introduced into Thailand around 400 years ago by Portuguese traders who imported them from South America. Prior to this, the heat element in Thai food had come from pepper and galangal.

There are several kinds of chile used in Thailand. Here I will introduce you to five of the most important varieties. The hottest is the *prik kee noo suan*, which translates as "mouse droppings" (the similarity is in the shape!). *Prik kee noo suan* chiles are green when young and ripen to red. When red, the taste is hotter, but the chiles have no aroma. When green they are milder (although still very hot for Western tastes), but have a noticeable aroma.

The chile which comes next on the hotness scale is *prik kee noo* (without the *suan*), which is called the birdseye chile or Thai chile in the West. It is at least an inch long and slightly less hot than the "mouse dropping," but still pretty fierce.

The third kind of chile is called *prik chee faa*. It can be either red or green and is about 3–4 inches in length. *Prik chee faa* are slightly less hot than the smaller varieties, but should still be handled with caution.

Prik haeng are large sun-dried red chiles similar in size to *prik chee faa*. They are deep maroon/red and need to be soaked, cut into pieces, then allowed to dry again before use.

The final chile is the *prik yuak*. It is large, pale yellow-green and shaped rather like the sweet bell peppers eaten in the West. If a recipe calls for *prik yuak* and you don't have any available, you can use a white Hungarian paprika chile or even a regular sweet bell pepper instead.

Thais believe that if you burn a chile covered in salt it will remove any "bad spirits" that may be around you. The Isaan people from northeast Thailand believe that eating very hot chiles will strengthen you, and the hotter you can eat the more "manly" you are.

SWEET BASIL AND HOLY BASIL

Several varieties of basil grow in Thailand, but sweet basil and holy basil are the ones familiar in the West because they travel well. Sweet basil is an annual herbaceous plant, the fresh leaves of which are either eaten raw or used as a flavoring in Thai cooking. It is not unlike the basil used in the Mediterranean. Thai or holy Basil has narrower leaves and is sometimes tinged with a reddish-purple color. It has a stronger taste than sweet basil, which is only released when cooked.

left
Prik kee noo chiles for sale by the bag.

below
Holy basil on the left and sweet basil on the right.

right
Selling *kapee* (shrimp paste). The price is per kilo (in Thai baht) and ranges from a cheap version made with offcuts of fish, through to the most expensive one that is made with good-quality shrimp.

SHRIMP PASTE

Kapee or shrimp paste is a pungent preserve used extensively in Thai cooking. It is made by pounding shrimp with salt and leaving them to decompose. *Kapee* smells fairly unpleasant when it is raw (some Thai farmers use it to keep monkeys off their crops!), but, as soon as you cook it, the overwhelming odor disappears. I often think that the smell has the same effect on an untrained nose as walking into a cheese shop does for a Thai person! *Kapee* is at the heart of many curry pastes, and can be used to flavor boiled rice. Mixed with other ingredients such as garlic, chile, fish sauce, and lemon juice it makes *nam prik,* a hot runny paste that is served with fried fish or as a dip for raw vegetables.

left
Fish drying in the sun.

right
Yellow chiles are more rare than the green and red varieties and are usually found in the south of Thailand. Yellow curry pastes use fresh turmeric for color and if yellow chiles are available, they are added, too. See page 155 for a recipe that uses yellow curry paste.

regional differences

What are the regional differences between Thai curries?

In common with most cuisines, Thai food is very local. Most dishes developed in specific regions because the people were using what grew around them there. The cuisine has developed on that basis.

Thailand can be divided into four geographical regions, each of which has its own culinary characteristics. The central plains, in which Bangkok is situated, are the most fertile part of the country and the most typically "Thai." Because communications are good and the region is the center of business and government, the central plains have absorbed cooking practices from all over the country. As a result, all the classic Thai curries are eaten in the area. They tend to lie somewhere in the middle on the hotness scale.

Northern Thailand consists of a series of upland valleys and is ethnically diverse, with hill tribes and a noticeable Burmese influence. The climate is too cool for coconut palms, so coconut oil is not a feature of local curries. The traditional frying medium used to be rendered pork fat, which gave northern food a special silky richness, but nowadays most people use vegetable oil. Curries from this fertile region are typically less hot than in the rest of the country. One possible reason for this is that ingredients were historically so plentiful in the area that there was no need to make very spicy food to make a little go a long way.

The northeast of Thailand is known as Isaan. It consists of a plateau about 300 meters (985 feet) above sea level and was very isolated and forested until the 19th century. The northeast has an extreme climate, with a long, dry season followed by frequent floods. The fertility of the soil in the region is not good, which may be why, in contrast to the north, its curries are often extremely hot. Food was often scarce and the spicier it was, the further it would go. Other features of northeastern cuisine include the use of glutinous, rather than long-grain, rice, small dried red chiles, and a fondness for fermented fish (*plaa raa*) as a seasoning.

Coconut palms grow all over in southern Thailand, so coconut cream and milk feature strongly in local curries. Fishing is the most important part of the economy and seafood is abundant. This part of the country was the first point of contact with traders from India and Arabia, so many of its curries show their influence, for instance in the use of turmeric. This is also the most Islamic part of Thailand —about a third of the population is Muslim—and there is a sharp distinction between the curries made by Muslims and Buddhists in the region. The former are usually cooked with ghee (clarified butter) or yogurt plus stock, whereas Buddhists use coconut cream. Curries in the south are quite hot and tend to incorporate yellow chiles and fiery birdseye chiles (*prik kee noo*, see page 16), rather than the long red ones used further north. And the cooking of the far south has a strong Malay influence.

What is the difference between wet and dry curries?

Some Thai curries use quite a lot of liquid, which can be coconut milk, stock, or water, and so have a soupy or stew-like consistency. They are, therefore, sometimes called wet curries. The idea is that the sauce will coat and cling to the rice served with them. Dry curries, such as Spicy Pork with Long Beans on page 105 and Hot Dry Beef Curry on page 113, have little or no liquid added after the paste has been fried.

making a thai curry

How do I structure a curry?

Most of the curries in this book are fried. This means that during the first stage, the relevant curry paste is gently fried in oil. This is usually vegetable oil, but some of the recipes call for the paste to be fried in the oily component of coconut cream (examples include the Shrimp Curry on page 134 and the Chicken Curry with Sour Bamboo Shoots on page 76). This entails first heating the coconut cream over a low heat until the solids and oil start to separate and will ensure that the paste fries properly. If the coconut cream hasn't separated, it will boil instead, which will not produce the desired taste. In Thailand, coconut cream is usually freshly made, so this is not a problem. The trouble with prepacked coconut cream is that it is often homogenized, which prevents it from separating properly. Try to buy non-homogenized coconut creams and milks. There are various brands available and the labels will give you the necessary information. If a recipe calls for the curry paste to be fried in coconut cream and you only have the homogenized kind, add a little vegetable oil to ensure the paste genuinely fries.

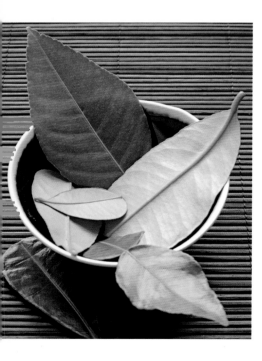

If you are making a fried curry, the second stage is usually to add the main ingredient (meat, fish, or vegetables) and fry for a few minutes. The third stage is to add the liquid, which will be coconut milk, stock, or water, depending on the recipe. It is important that you follow the correct sequence if you want your curries to taste authentic.

The other kind of curry popular in Thailand, particularly in the north, is boiled rather than fried. This involves dissolving the curry paste in the cooking liquid rather than in oil. A good example is Fish Curry with Kaffir Lime on page 125.

What kind of oil should I use to fry the curry paste?

I recommend that you use peanut or sunflower oils, which have very little taste of their own and therefore do not mask the delicate flavors of the other ingredients. Strong-tasting frying mediums, such as olive oil, should be avoided.

Can you reheat a curry?

When curry is sold as street food in Thailand, cold curry is poured over hot rice, so warming up the curry. In Thai homes, a big pot of curry is cooked in the morning and reheated for lunch and for the evening meal. At other times of the day it can be served with hot rice to warm it up.

What can you do to intensify the flavor of a curry?

Adding lemongrass or lime leaves to the stock used in the cooking of a curry will give it a stronger and more fragrant flavor. Another way to perk up a bland tasting curry is to use *nam pra prik*. To make enough to accompany one curry, combine 1 tablespoon fish sauce, the juice from 1/4 lemon and 1 finely chopped small red chile in a little bowl. Most homes have *nam pra prik* made up and ready at hand for those who prefer their curries to have a more intense taste.

left
Kaffir lime leaves.

right
Floating street food in Bangkok. The calls of "curry noodles coming now!" entice people to the canal side to eat.

curry paste ingredients

These ingredients are used for stage 1 of cooking.

CARDAMOM
A warm spice encased in green, black, or creamy beige pods—green being the most common. Whole pods are used to flavor rice and meat dishes, particularly in the Muslim-influenced south. The pods themselves should not be eaten.

CHILES
See page 16 ("What are the other key ingredients in Thai curries?") for the common types of chiles.

CINNAMON
Available as sticks or ground, cinnamon has a woody

aroma with a warm, fragrant flavor. Cinnamon trees are native to Sri Lanka.

CLOVES
This sweet, warming spice is used in both savory and sweet dishes, but like most dried spices, its use in Thai cooking is largely confined to Muslim dishes in the south.

CORIANDER
This herb, the leaves of which are also known as Chinese parsley or cilantro, is widely featured in Thai dishes and as a garnish. Leaves, seeds, stems and the roots are all used. See also page 15 ("Why is the combination of coriander, lemongrass, and garlic so Thai?").

GALANGAL

Galangal is a rhizome plant that looks rather like ginger but has pink root tips and a unique, pungent flavor. In the West, ginger is often used to replace it, but the dishes won't taste the same.

GARLIC

Thai garlic cloves are small with thin, papery skin, which we often don't bother to peel away before use, but if you are using Western garlic you should peel it. See also page 15 ("Why is the combination of coriander, lemongrass, and garlic so Thai?").

GINGER

The root of this tuber should be peeled, then sliced, finely chopped, or shredded. As with most herbs and foods, it tastes better fresh. Fresh ginger is known for its warm, pungent flavor. A native of Southeast Asia, it is used in many intriguing spice combinations.

KAFFIR LIME

This knobbly lime is roughly the same size and shape as the common lime, but has little juice. The peel is often used in recipes for curry pastes.

KAFFIR LIME LEAVES

The dark green, glossy leaves of the kaffir lime impart a pungent lemon-lime flavor to dishes. They are available in some supermarkets and Oriental stores. The fresh leaves keep well and can be frozen.

KRACHAI (CHINESE KEY)

This annual has aromatic rhizomes and yellow-brown roots, and is used as a flavoring. It also has a medicinal value as an aid to digestion.

LEMONGRASS

Fresh lemongrass is common to many dishes throughout Southeast Asia. Its rich lemon flavor combines well with other wet spices. Lemongrass is also available dried but tastes inferior. See also page 15 ("Why is the combination of coriander, lemongrass, and garlic so Thai?").

NUTMEG

Another spice used in some recipes from the south of Thailand, nutmeg comes in the form of dark brown or white "nuts." These should be kept whole in an airtight container and grated when needed. Ground nutmeg does not keep.

left
Coriander roots.

below
Kaffir limes.

right
Krachai (chinese key).

PEPPERCORNS

The white, green, and black peppercorns are berries from the same plant, picked at different stages of maturity. They are used whole and ground.

SHALLOTS

The shallot is a member of the onion family, but it has a sweeter and milder taste. Thai shallots are so sweet that they are sometimes used in desserts! When buying shallots, go for the smaller ones. Larger specimens tend to be too oniony.

SHRIMP PASTE

This is a strongly flavored paste used to flavor rice and curries. See page 17 ("What are the other key ingredients in Thai curries?").

STAR ANISE

These are star-shaped, licorice-flavored pods indigenous to China. Like cardamom, the pods are used whole during cooking and should not be eaten.

TAMARIND

An acidic-tasting tropical fruit which resembles a bean pod. It gives a sharp flavor to curries. Tamarind is sold dried or pulped, and needs to be dissolved in hot water to extract the juice (see page 83).

TURMERIC

Another member of the ginger family, this can occasionally be found fresh in Oriental stores, but more frequently in powdered form. When the whole spice is peeled or scraped, a rich golden root is revealed. Turmeric adds a distinctive flavor and rich yellow color to dishes.

liquid ingredients

These ingredients are the liquid element of Thai curries and are usually added in stage 2 of cooking.

FISH SAUCE (*NAM PLA*)
This is the basic savory flavoring of Thai cooking, for which there is no substitute. Available bottled in Oriental stores, it imparts a very distinctive salty flavor. It is made by pounding small fresh fish and/or shrimp with salt and leaving the mixture to ferment for a year or so. The resulting liquid is then strained and bottled. The best *nam pla* has a light whiskey color and a refreshing taste.

Darker versions are often heavy and bitter—I tend to avoid them. Darkness in a fish sauce is also a sign that the bottle has been open too long. If your *nam pla* has changed color significantly, you should replace it. Commercial fish sauces vary quite a lot in taste and saltiness, so experiment until you find a brand you like. You should also adjust the amount you use in a recipe according to its saltiness. Use taste as your guide. As ever, you are aiming to make sure the flavors are balanced.

SOY SAUCE (*SIEW*)

Of the two types of soy sauce, the light version is thin, with a clear, delicate salty flavor and is the one most commonly used in cooking. Dark soy sauce adds color as well as flavor to a dish. Use Thai, Malay, or Vietnamese soy sauce for cooking; the Japanese version is too dark and has the wrong flavor.

BEAN SAUCE (*TOW JIEW*)

Tow jiew is a thickish sauce made from crushed, fermented, and salted soybeans mixed with flour and spices. Varieties are made using both black and yellow beans, although the black bean kind is more common. *Tow jiew* is sold in jars or cans. Once opened, it should be kept in the fridge.

STOCK OR BROTH

When a recipe calls for stock or broth, the finished dish will be much better if you make it yourself, rather than using store-bought varieties. The way I make stocks is extremely simple. For a chicken, beef, or pork stock, I place the bones in a large pot with no other ingredients, cover them with water, and simmer for about 2 hours, skimming off any impurities as they rise to the surface. For a vegetable stock, I place 1 onion, 2 carrots, and 2 celery stalks in a large pot of water, together with some coriander (cilantro) stalks and a few black peppercorns, and simmer them until the liquid has reduced by about a fifth.

COCONUT MILK

For all these recipes, I have assumed you will use canned coconut milk. If the recipe requires coconut cream, open the can without shaking it, and separate the thicker white cream from the transparent liquid, scooping it out with a ladle.

Many people think that coconut milk is made from the watery juice inside the coconut. In fact, it is made by grating the white flesh, mixing it with warm water, then pressing it. The milk is used extensively in Thai curries and desserts. Dairy milk and products were completely unknown in Thailand until recently—they are not used in Thai cooking, except in the Muslim dishes of the south. Instead, Thais use coconut milk and coconut cream. Both are marketed worldwide in cartons, cans, and blocks, and now in powdered form. If you can find grated coconut (unsweetened, not the dried kind), you can also make coconut milk with it, by mixing it with warm water and squeezing it. Making your own milk from the coconut flesh is hard work, but it does give a better flavor. It is worth trying if you want to make a really special curry.

making curry pastes

For the true taste of a Thai curry, curry paste needs to be freshly made, not bought. It is best done by pounding the ingredients using a stone mortar and pestle. In Thailand, a good mortar and pestle will be handed down from mother to daughter over several generations. In the old days, each ingredient was prepared individually before being pounded together to achieve the correct consistency. Dried red chiles, for example, have to be soaked, sliced into small pieces, then pounded with coarse salt to break down the chile skin and achieve the correct texture. There is no doubt that, prepared this way, you get the freshest taste, and it is an easy matter to alter the balance of flavors by adjusting the quantities of the different ingredients—more chile, less pepper, etc.

However, preparing the paste in this way is time-consuming and hard work. Until about 60 years ago, it was the only way to prepare curry paste and it would only keep for two days or so. My great aunt used to sell curry pastes in the market. Her husband, a sailor in the Thai navy, was away for months at a time. He knew that it was always a problem to prepare and keep curry paste on board, so he developed a technique to make a paste that could be dried and stored for use at a later date. This he subsequently developed into a business, under the brand name *Tan Jai*. Their first customer was the Thai navy! Later, it became hugely popular with Thai students going abroad to study. Sadly, the brand no longer exists, although this type of product is widely available. In the West, only the best-known curries (green, red, massaman, and penang) are found, but these recipes will show you how to make your own.

How to make authentic Thai curry pastes

The preparation of the curry pastes is the same for each curry. The ingredients should be ground using a mortar and pestle. Start with the hardest ingredient then add the other ingredients one at a time. I usually start with the chiles and sea salt—the coarse salt helps to cut through the chile skin. As you add each ingredient, check the aroma of the paste to see how the new ingredient is balancing with the previous ones. This will ensure that you don't add too much or too little of any ingredient. You are aiming for a harmonious blend with no one flavor dominating.

Any leftover paste will keep in the fridge for two or three days. The best way to keep it fresh is to wrap it in plastic wrap and place it in an airtight container. You can also freeze your curry pastes—they may lose a little flavor but they will still taste better than store-bought pastes. Wrap in two-tablespoon portions so you can use as needed.

With practice, you can expect to grind a curry paste in about thirty minutes. It is hard work, but it can be a great stress-buster and the results are definitely worth it. The alternative is to use a blender. This will produce inferior pastes, but they will probably still be better than ready-made ones. If you do decide to use a blender, lubricate the ingredients with water rather than oil or you will end up with a gluey ball.

Note: If dried red chiles are required, always prepare them in this way: slice lengthways, remove the seeds, cut into ½-inch pieces, soak until soft, then let dry before grinding.

For the eight key curry pastes, I have given the amount of garlic and shallot by weight, not quantity, since sizes vary widely. This way, you can reproduce the balance of flavors exactly as I make it, and then adjust as necessary to suit your own taste.

left
Soaking dried chiles.

right
These stone mortar and pestle last for years and are handed down through the generations. It always amazes me that there is still a market for them!

below right
A mortar and pestle maker at Ang Sila, a small fishing village near Pattaya where stone mortar and pestles have been produced for hundreds of years.

curry paste recipes

Green Curry Paste
GAENG KEOW WAN

Makes roughly 20 tablespoons (1¼ cups)

3½ ounces (roughly 50–60) small fresh
   green chiles
1 teaspoon sea salt (or kosher salt)
2½ ounces shallots, peeled and finely chopped
   (about 6–7 tbsp.)
3 ounces garlic, peeled and finely chopped
   (about 10 tbsp.)
3 tablespoons finely chopped fresh galangal
4 lemongrass stalks, finely chopped
1 tablespoon finely chopped kaffir lime peel
1 teaspoon finely chopped cilantro root
2 tablespoons white peppercorns
1 tablespoon coriander seeds, toasted
1 tablespoon cumin seeds, toasted
1 tablespoon shrimp paste

Red Curry Paste
GAENG PET

Makes roughly 28 tablespoons (1¾ cups)

10 large dried red chiles
$^2/_3$ ounce shallots, peeled and finely chopped
   (about 2 tbsp.)
1½ ounces garlic, peeled and finely chopped
   (about 5 tbsp.)
2 tablespoons chopped fresh galangal
4 lemongrass stalks, finely chopped
2 teaspoons finely chopped kaffir lime peel
1 tablespoon finely chopped cilantro root
1 teaspoon white peppercorns
2 teaspoons coriander seeds
1 teaspoon cumin seeds
1 tablespoon shrimp paste

Massaman Curry Paste
GAENG MASSAMAN

Makes roughly 25 tablespoons (about 1½ cups)

7 large dried red chiles
1 teaspoon sea salt
1 ounce shallots, peeled and finely chopped
  (about 2½–3 tbsp.)
1½ ounces garlic, peeled and finely chopped
  (about 5 tbsp.)
2 tablespoons finely chopped fresh galangal,
  toasted until brown
4 lemongrass stalks, finely chopped and
  toasted until brown
2 tablespoons finely chopped cilantro root
1 tablespoon white peppercorns
1 tablespoon coriander seeds, toasted
1 tablespoon cumin seeds, toasted
8 whole cardamom pods, toasted, husks
  removed and seeds scraped out
1 small nutmeg, toasted, break the shell off and
  use the meat inside
½ teaspoon ground cinnamon
8 cloves, toasted
1 tablespoon shrimp paste

Penang Curry Paste
GAENG PENANG

Makes roughly 12 tablespoons (¾ cup)

5 large dried red chiles
½ teaspoon sea salt (or kosher salt)
⅔ ounce shallots, peeled and finely chopped
  (about 2 tbsp.)
1½ ounces garlic, peeled and finely chopped
  (about 5 tbsp.)
1 tablespoon finely chopped fresh galangal
2 lemongrass stalks, finely chopped
1 tablespoon finely chopped kaffir lime peel
1 tablespoon finely chopped cilantro root
1 teaspoon white peppercorns
2 teaspoons coriander seeds, toasted
  until brown
1 teaspoon cumin seeds, toasted until brown
2 tablespoons roasted peanuts
1 tablespoon shrimp paste

Jungle Curry Paste
GAENG PA

Makes roughly 12 tablespoons (¾ cup)

10 large dried red chiles
1 teaspoon sea salt (or kosher salt)
**²/₃ ounce shallots, peeled and finely chopped
(about 2 tbsp.)**
**1½ ounces garlic, peeled and finely chopped
(about 5 tbsp.)**
2 tablespoons finely chopped fresh galangal
4 lemongrass stalks, finely chopped
2 teaspoons coriander seeds
1 tablespoon shrimp paste

Kua Curry Paste
GAENG KUA

Makes roughly 14 tablespoons (a scant cup)

10 small dried red chiles
5 large dried red chiles
1 teaspoon sea salt (or kosher salt)
**²/₃ ounce shallots, peeled and finely chopped
(about 2 tbsp.)**
**1¾ ounces garlic, peeled and finely chopped
(about 6 tbsp.)**
1 tablespoon finely chopped fresh galangal
4 lemongrass stalks, finely chopped
1 tablespoon finely chopped kaffir lime peel
1 tablespoon white peppercorns
**1 tablespoon finely chopped fresh turmeric
(if unavailable, use the same quantity of
ground turmeric)**

Home-style Curry Paste
GAENG BHAN

Makes roughly 15 tablespoons (a scant cup)

**3½ ounces (roughly 70–80) small dried
   red chiles**
½ teaspoon sea salt (or kosher salt)
**3½ ounces garlic, peeled and finely chopped
   (about ¾ cup)**
2 tablespoons finely chopped fresh galangal
4 lemongrass stalks, finely chopped
3 tablespoons finely chopped kaffir lime peel
1 tablespoon shrimp paste

Orange Curry Paste
GAENG SOM

Makes roughly 10 tablespoons (about ²/₃ cup)

**1¾ ounces (roughly 30–40) small dried
   red chiles**
½ teaspoon sea salt (or kosher salt)
**²/₃ ounce shallots, peeled and finely chopped
   (about 2 tbsp.)**
**1 ounce garlic, peeled and finely chopped
   (about 4 tbsp.)**
**2 tablespoons finely chopped fresh turmeric
   (if unavailable, use the same quantity of
   ground turmeric)**
1 tablespoon shrimp paste

accompaniments

Curry Powder
PONG KARI

Not so much of an accompaniment as a vital ingredient in several recipes in this book. This recipe makes roughly 10 tablespoons and can be stored in an airtight container for up to one year.

Whole herbs and spices
2 teaspoons cloves
2-inch piece cinnamon stick
2 teaspoons fennel seeds
4–5 bay leaves

Ground spices
2 tablespoons ground cumin
5 tablespoons ground coriander
2 teaspoons ground turmeric
2 teaspoons paprika

Mix the whole herbs and spices together in a dry wok or frying pan. Stir-fry over medium heat for 1 minute or until their aroma starts to fill the air. Allow the spices to cool, then grind as finely as possible using a mortar and pestle or spice grinder. Mix in the ground spices and stir well.

Noodles and Rice

There are no rules as to whether you have noodles or rice with a curry; it is really a matter of personal preference.

Dried noodles usually need to be soaked for about 20 minutes before they can be cooked and drained. They are cooked either by immersing them in boiling water for 2 or 3 seconds or by stir-frying (read the package instructions for details). The main noodle types are as follows:

THIN RICE NOODLES (*SEN MEE*)
A small wiry-looking noodle made from rice flour. Usually sold dried and labeled rice vermicelli.

LARGE RICE NOODLES (*SEN YAI*)
A broad, flat white noodle made from rice flour. When sold fresh, it is rather sticky and the strands need to be pulled apart before cooking. *Sen yai* is also sold dried, as rice sticks.

VERMICELLI NOODLES (*WUN SEN*)
A very thin translucent noodle made from soybean flour. Only available dried.

EGG NOODLES (*BA MEE*)
The many varieties of egg noodles, from flat, broad ribbons to long, narrow strands, are available both fresh and dried.

RICE (*KHAO*)
Thai rice is long grained and jasmine scented. It is sold abroad as "Thai fragrant rice." To make enough for four to six people, first rinse $2^2/_3$ cups of rice in cold water at least three times until the water runs clear. Then place the rice in a heavy-bottomed pan and add $2^2/_3$ cups of water. Place the lid on the pan and quickly bring to a boil. Remove the lid and continue boiling, stirring vigorously, until the water level is below the surface of the rice. Finally, turn the heat down as low as possible, replace the lid on the pan, and steam for 20 minutes—if the lid doesn't fit tightly, cover the pan with a layer of aluminum foil to ensure a good seal. The alternative is to buy a rice cooker; they are cheap, easy to use, and will provide you with perfect rice whenever you need it.

left
Egg noodles (*ba mee*).

right
A vendor brewing and selling fresh coffee. Not so long ago, before so many of Bangkok's canals were built over, this was a very common sight in the city. The vendor would punt his boat along the canals and people would order coffee from their porches on the canal side. Today, this still takes place, but it's mostly in the far suburbs of Bangkok where the extensive network of canals and rivers is still in everyday use.

far right
Hot tea makes a good accompaniment to curry; jasmine tea is the most popular choice.

What to drink with a Thai curry?

Most people will drink water. Others prefer black or white iced coffee or tea made very strong and sweet which rounds off the meal, almost like a dessert. Traditionally, alcohol is only drunk with snacks, particularly with *yam* (a spicy Thai salad, not the starchy African vegetable!). It is not usual to drink alcohol with the main evening meal.

pickles and relishes

Ajart should be treated like a side dish. It goes particularly well with dry or rich curries that do not have vegetables included, such as Chicken Massaman Curry (page 80), Massaman Lamb Curry (page 117), Lamb Curry with Rice (page 59), and Curry Coconut Rice (page 60). *Ajart* is also used as a dip for savory snacks like Corn Cakes (page 44). This recipe serves 4–6 people. It doesn't keep well as the vegetables go soft; eat on the same day.

Fresh Vegetable Pickles
AJART

1 cup rice vinegar
4 tablespoons sugar
1 teaspoon salt
1 large red chile, sliced
1 large green chile, sliced
1 pound (total weight) cucumber, shallots, carrots, sliced

Heat the vinegar in a pan. Add the sugar and salt and stir to dissolve. Allow the mixture to cool. Place the sliced vegetables in a bowl and cover with the vinegar. Set aside for 30 minutes, then serve.

Various fruits and vegetables can be pickled, either in salted water or in a mixture of salt, sugar, and vinegar. They are used in the cooking method of some of the curry recipes in this book and are also good as accompaniments to the curries—it's largely a matter of personal preference as to which ones you choose to serve!

Salted Eggs
KAI KEM

8 duck eggs
7 ounces (¾ cup) salt
3 cups water

Place the eggs in their shells in a canning jar. Heat the salt and water in a saucepan until the salt has dissolved. Allow the mixture to cool, then pour it over the eggs in the jar. Seal the jar and set aside for 3 weeks, after which the eggs can be boiled or fried.

Pickled Garlic
KING DONG

1 pound garlic, peeled
2 cups rice vinegar
1 cup sugar
2 tablespoons salt

Place the garlic cloves in a bowl, cover with water, and soak for 1 hour. Drain and allow to dry for another hour. Heat the vinegar in a pan, add the sugar and salt, and stir to dissolve. Let the mixture cool. Place the garlic in a canning jar, pour the vinegar over the garlic, and seal the jar. Set aside for 3–4 weeks. Do not refrigerate until after the jar is opened.

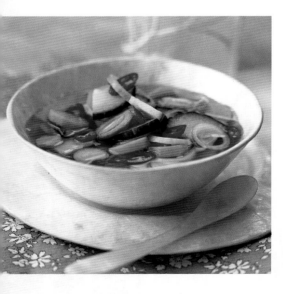

Pickled Ginger
KRATIAM DONG

1 pound fresh young ginger, peeled and cut into thin slices
2 cups rice vinegar
2 cups sugar
2 tablespoons salt

Place the ginger in a bowl and rinse in water.
Drain and set aside. Heat the vinegar in a pan,
add the sugar and salt, and stir to dissolve.
Allow the mixture to cool. Place the ginger
in a canning jar,
pour the vinegar
over it, and seal the
jar. Leave for 3 weeks.
Do not refrigerate
until after the jar
is opened.

SNACKS AND
ONE-DISH MEALS

Bangkok People
CHAO KRUNG

The serenity of Buddhist temples is in stark contrast to the overhead Skytrain, the gleaming new underground metro, the water taxis hurtling down the Chao Phraya River and through the canals, and the uncountable numbers of cars, buses, and trucks seething around the city in a huge riot of noise and color. Welcome to the all-day rush hour of Bangkok. As in most Asian cities, people lead a frantic lifestyle, striving to earn a living and spending two or three hours every day traveling to and from work. It is an exhausting day, after which cooking is an effort, one that you can gladly leave to others —especially when street food is as good and as cheap as it is here.

Pork Satay with Peanut Curry Sauce
MOO SATAY

Satay was introduced from Malaysia—I remember when I was young the people selling satay on street stalls were never Thai! But satay is now synonymous with Thai food. You can make these with chicken, beef, pork, or jumbo shrimp. You can also serve thin slices of white bread which can also be dipped into the peanut sauce.

1 pound lean boneless pork, cut lengthways into strips about ¾ inch wide
2 tablespoons oil
2 tablespoons palm sugar (or brown sugar)

for the curry paste marinade
2 teaspoons coriander seeds, toasted
2 teaspoons cumin seeds, toasted
1 lemongrass stalk, finely sliced
1 tablespoon finely sliced fresh galangal
1 teaspoon chopped kaffir lime peel
1 teaspoon ground turmeric
1 teaspoon salt

for the peanut curry dipping sauce
2 tablespoons peanut oil
1 tablespoon Penang Curry Paste (see page 29)
½ cup coconut milk
½ cup chicken stock
1 tablespoon sugar
1 teaspoon salt
2 tablespoons lime juice
1 cup roasted peanuts, crushed

Wooden skewers, soaked in cold water for 30 minutes

First make the marinade. Place the coriander seeds in a mortar and grind to a powder, then add the other ingredients one at a time, grinding each one into the mixture to form a paste.

Place the pork, your freshly made marinade, oil, and palm sugar in a bowl, mix thoroughly, cover, and let marinate in the fridge for 3–5 hours.

To make the dipping sauce, heat the oil in a pan. Add the Penang Curry Paste, stir well, and cook for few seconds. Stir in the coconut milk, stock, sugar, salt, and lime juice and stir to blend. Cook for 2 minutes, stirring constantly. Add the peanuts, stirring, then pour the sauce into a bowl and set aside.

Thread two pieces of marinated pork onto each skewer, then grill, broil, or barbecue the satays for about 5 minutes on each side until the meat is cooked through. Serve with the peanut curry dipping sauce.

Spicy Coconut Cakes
TOD MAN MAPRAO

Coconut has many uses in Thai cooking—here it is mixed with curry paste to make a savory snack.

1 tablespoon Red Curry Paste (see page 28)
7 ounces grated fresh coconut
4 fresh kaffir lime leaves, finely sliced
1/2 teaspoon salt
1 teaspoon sugar
Oil, for deep-frying

Place the curry paste, coconut, lime leaves, salt, and sugar in a mortar and pound together to form a paste.

Heat the oil in wok or deep pan. Take 2 tablespoons of the paste and form into patties about 1/2 inch thick. Carefully lower into the hot oil and cook until golden brown. Serve with Fresh Vegetable Pickles (see page 34).

Fried Sweet Potato and Chicken Cakes
TOD MAN GAI

1 pound sweet potato, peeled, boiled until soft,
  then mashed
8 ounces chicken fillets, very finely chopped
1 tablespoon Massaman Curry Paste
  (see page 29)
1 egg
1 teaspoon salt
1 tablespoon cornstarch
3 scallions, finely chopped
Oil, for deep-frying

for the dipping sauce
3 tablespoons water
4 tablespoons sugar
1 tablespoon palm sugar
2 teaspoons salt
2 tablespoons tamarind water (see page 83)

First make the dipping sauce. Heat the water in a small pan, then add the remaining ingredients and simmer until a thick syrup forms. Set aside.

To make the cakes, place all the ingredients, except the oil, in a bowl and mix well. Wet your hands and form the mixture into patties about 2 inches across and 1/2 inch thick. Heat the oil in a wok or pan. Lower in the patties and fry until golden brown. Remove, drain on paper towels and serve with the dipping sauce.

Shrimp and Coconut Cakes with Plum Sauce
TOD MAN KUNG

Preserved plums have a salty and sour taste. You can buy them in bottles from Oriental stores.

10 ounces peeled raw shrimp, deveined and
   finely chopped
3 ounces grated fresh coconut
1 tablespoon Red Curry Paste (see page 28)
3 scallions, finely sliced
Handful of cilantro leaves, finely chopped
1 teaspoon salt
Oil, for deep-frying

for the plum sauce
2 preserved plums
½ cup rice vinegar
½ cup sugar
2 small fresh red chiles, finely chopped

First make the sauce. Use a fork to scrape the plum flesh from the pit. Pour the vinegar into a pan and heat gently. Add the sugar and the plum flesh, stir to dissolve the sugar, then simmer until a thin syrup forms. Pour into a bowl. add the chiles, and set aside.

Place the shrimp and grated coconut in a food processor and pulse to form a smooth paste. Transfer to a large bowl. Add the curry paste, scallions, cilantro, and salt. Knead the mixture, then shape into patties about 2 inches across and ½ inch thick.

Heat the oil in a wok or deep pan. Carefully lower in the shrimp cakes and fry until golden. Remove and drain on paper towels. Serve with the plum sauce.

right
Shrimp and Coconut
Cakes with Plum Sauce

Corn Cakes
TOD MAN KHAO POD

One of the best vegetarian Thai snacks. Serve with Fresh Vegetable Pickles (see page 34).

Kernels from 4–5 uncooked ears of corn
1 tablespoon Curry Powder (see page 32)
2 tablespoons rice flour
3 tablespoons all-purpose flour
1 teaspoon salt
Oil, for deep-frying

Mix together all the ingredients, except the oil, in a bowl, stirring well to form a thick mixture.

Heat the oil in a wok or deep pan. Take a tablespoon of the mixture, form it into a small cake, then carefully lower it into the hot oil. Deep-fry until golden brown, then remove from the oil and drain on paper towels. Repeat until all the mixture is used up. Let the cakes cool, then serve.

Seafood Toast
KANOM PANG TALAY

It's best to use bread that's a little bit dry, maybe a day old; too fresh and it will soak up too much oil. If you only have very fresh bread, put it in a warm oven first to dry slightly.

6 slices of white bread
4 ounces raw shrimp, peeled and deveined
4 ounces white fish fillets, any bones and skin removed
4 ounces small squid, cut into small pieces
2 eggs
1 tablespoon light soy sauce
¹/₂ teaspoon salt
1 tablespoon Red Curry Paste (see page 28)
5 tablespoons white sesame seeds
Oil, for deep-frying

Trim the crusts from the bread so that each slice is square. Cut each slice across the diagonals to make four triangles.

Place the shrimp, fish, and squid into a food processor or blender along with the eggs, soy sauce, salt, and curry paste. Blend to a smooth paste and spread evenly on the pieces of bread. Top with sesame seeds.

Heat the oil in a wok or frying pan. Carefully fry the toasts, a few at a time, until golden all over. Drain on paper towels and serve hot.

Vegetable Fritters with Curry Paste
PAK CHUP RANG TOD

Any selection of hard vegetables will work well for this snack. Taro (see picture below) is a tuber that should be treated like potato—you can boil, bake, or fry it. It is also used in a dessert called *gaeng buad,* where it is combined with coconut and palm sugar to make a sweet soup.

Oil, for deep-frying
1 handful courgettes, diagonally sliced
1 handful green papaya, halved lengthways
1 handful baby sweetcorn
1 handful carrots, halved lengthways
1 handful cauliflower florets
1 handful taro, halved lengthways
1 handful pumpkin, halved lengthways
1 handful sweet potato, halved lengthways

for the batter
½ tablespoon Home-style Curry Paste
  (see page 31)
¾ cup plain flour
½ teaspoon salt
2 eggs
½ teaspoon sugar
¾ cup water

for the dipping sauce
4 tablespoons light soy sauce
1 teaspoon sugar
1 teaspoon finely chopped ginger
1 scallion, finely sliced

First make the dipping sauce. Place all the ingredients in a bowl and stir well.

To make the batter, place the curry paste, flour, and salt in a bowl and mix well. Break the eggs into the bowl, add the sugar, and mix thoroughly. Gradually pour in the water, whisking constantly.

Heat the oil in a wok or deep pan. Dip each vegetable into the batter, then carefully lower into the hot oil. Deep-fry until golden brown. Remove from the oil, drain on paper towels, arrange on a large dish, and serve with the sauce.

Spicy Beef Balls
NUA TOD

This might look like a kind of burger but trust me, it tastes much more interesting!

left
Spicy Beef Balls

1 pound ground beef
1 large onion, finely chopped
1 tablespoon Massaman Curry Paste
  (see page 29)
2 eggs, beaten
2 tablespoons fish sauce
1/2 teaspoon salt
1 teaspoon sugar
3 tablespoons unsalted peanuts, chopped
Oil, for deep-frying
Lemon wedges, for serving

Place all the ingredients, except the oil, in a large bowl and mix well until the mixture is smooth. Wet your hands and shape the mixture into golf-size balls. Set aside.

Heat the oil in a wok or deep pan. Prepare a tray lined with paper towels to drain the beef balls. Lower the balls, a few at a time, into the hot oil and deep-fry until golden brown. Remove and drain on the paper towels. Serve hot with lemon wedges.

Noodles with Curry Sauce
GUEYTEOW GAENG JAY

This is a little unusual, as all the ingredients are broiled, giving the dish a smoky flavor.

6 ounces fresh egg noodles
3 cups bean sprouts
3 ounces long beans, sliced into 1-inch pieces
Cilantro leaves, for garnishing

for the curry sauce
4 large fresh red chiles
6 large garlic cloves, peeled
2 medium onions, peeled
4 medium tomatoes
2 tablespoons light soy sauce
2 tablespoons lime juice
2 teaspoons sugar
1/2 teaspoon salt

First make the sauce. Wrap the chiles, garlic, onions, and tomatoes together in aluminum foil. Place under a medium broiler and cook until they begin to soften (about 15–20 minutes). Remove from the foil, then pound in a mortar for about 1 minute to form a paste. Add the soy sauce, lime juice, sugar, and salt, stir well, then pour into a serving bowl and set aside.

Blanch the noodles in a large pot of boiling water, drain, and pile onto a serving dish. Blanch the bean sprouts and long beans in the same water. Arrange the bean sprouts and long beans on the noodles. Ladle the curry sauce over the noodles, garnish with cilantro, and serve.

Stir-fried Beef Noodles with Curry Paste

MEE SUA

Noodles were introduced into Thai cuisine from China some time ago. The Chinese way was to serve them quite plain but they are more spicy now and most definitely Thai!

2 tablespoons oil
4 small garlic cloves, finely chopped
1 tablespoon Red Curry Paste (see page 28)
1 pound beef tenderloin steak, thinly sliced
**5 nests of egg noodles, soaked in cold water for
   15 minutes and drained**
2 tablespoons fish sauce
2 tablespoons light soy sauce
2 cups bean sprouts
2 carrots, cut into fine matchsticks
2 large fresh red chiles, diagonally sliced
2 scallions, chopped into 1-inch pieces

Heat the oil in a wok, add the garlic, and stir-fry until golden. Add the curry paste and stir well. Add the beef and cook for about 5 minutes, stirring well. Add the remaining ingredients, and cook for a few minutes more. Mix well, then serve.

right
**Stir-fried Beef Noodles
with Curry Paste**

Curry-flavored Beef Noodles

GUEYTEOW NUA SAP

Tang chi is made from hard vegetable stalks, mainly cabbage stems, which are preserved in salt.

5 lettuce leaves (any variety)
3 tablespoons oil
8 ounces rice ribbon noodles
1 teaspoon dark soy sauce
2 garlic cloves, finely chopped
½ cup ground beef
2 tablespoons light soy sauce
1 tablespoon Curry Powder (see page 32)
**1 teaspoon cornstarch blended with
   ½ cup water**
**1 teaspoon store-bought *tang chi* (preserved
   vegetable)**
1 teaspoon sugar
Cilantro leaves, for garnishing

Arrange the lettuce leaves on a serving dish. Heat 1 tablespoon of the oil in a wok or frying pan. Add the noodles, stir, then add the dark soy sauce and stir-fry until the noodles are cooked. Tip onto the lettuce and set aside.

Pour the remaining oil into the wok, add the garlic, and fry until golden. Add the ground beef, light soy sauce, and curry powder and stir well, cooking for about 5 minutes. Stir in the cornstarch mixture and add the *tang chi* and sugar. Pour it over the noodles, garnish with cilantro, and serve.

Spicy Crispy Noodles
MEE KROP

Mee krop has a sweet taste and is very popular in America; it is always on the menu in Thai restaurants there and is eaten as a dish in its own right, whereas in Thailand it would be served with a curry. Dried shrimp (*gung haeng*) is a dry, salty flavoring that is made by boiling and peeling shrimp and leaving them out in the sun to dry.

Oil, for deep-frying
8 ounces rice vermicelli

for the sauce
2 tablespoons oil
6 ounces firm tofu, cut into ¼-inch cubes
²/₃ cup dried shrimp (*gung haeng*)
1 tablespoon Orange Curry Paste
** (see page 31)**
3 tablespoons fish sauce
2 tablespoons palm sugar (or brown sugar)
2 tablespoons tamarind water (see page 83)

for the garnish
2 tablespoons oil
1 egg, lightly beaten
1 cup bean sprouts
3 scallions, cut into 1-inch slivers
2 medium fresh red chiles, seeded and
** finely sliced**
20 cloves of Pickled Garlic, finely sliced across
** (see page 34)**

Heat the oil in a wok over medium heat. Add the dry noodles and deep-fry until golden brown and crisp. Drain and set aside.

To make the sauce, heat the 2 tablespoons oil in the wok, add the tofu, and stir-fry until crisp. Remove and set aside. Stir-fry the dried shrimp until crisp. Remove and set aside. Add the curry paste to the wok, stir well, then add the fish sauce, palm sugar, and tamarind water. Continue stirring until the mixture begins to caramelize. Add the reserved tofu and dried shrimp, stir quickly, then remove from the heat.

In another wok or small pan, heat 2 tablespoons oil for the garnish. Drip in the egg mixture to make little ribbons of cooked egg. Drain and set aside.

Return the wok with the sauce to the heat and crumble in the crispy noodles, mixing gently. Transfer to a serving dish, sprinkle with the bean sprouts, scallions, cooked egg, sliced chile, and pickled garlic, and serve.

Thai Fried Noodles with Crab
MEE PAD BOO

4 tablespoons oil
1 tablespoon Massaman Curry Paste
  (see page 29)
2 large eggs
8 ounces rice vermicelli, soaked in water for
  30 minutes and drained
4 scallions, finely sliced
8 ounces fresh white crabmeat, shredded
2 cups bean sprouts
4 tablespoons fish sauce
2 tablespoons sugar
2 tablespoons chopped roasted peanuts
4 tablespoons lime juice
Cilantro leaves, for garnishing

Heat the oil in a wok or frying pan, then stir in the curry paste. Break the eggs into the wok, cook for 1 minute, and stir.

Add the noodles, stir well, then add the remaining ingredients in order, stirring well between each addition. Ladle onto a plate, garnish with cilantro, and serve.

right
Thai Fried Noodles
with Crab

Southern Curry Noodles
GUEYTEOW KAEK

1 pound boneless pork, cut into 1-inch cubes
2 tablespoons oil
5 shallots, finely sliced
4 garlic cloves, finely chopped
1 tablespoon Penang Curry Paste (see page 29)
2 cups coconut milk
2 tablespoons fish sauce
2 teaspoons sugar
2 tablespoons *chipo* (preserved radish),
  finely chopped
2 tablespoons ground roasted peanuts
8 ounces rice vermicelli, soaked in cold water
  for 30 minutes and drained
2 hard-boiled eggs, peeled and quartered
Cilantro leaves, for garnishing

Place the pork in a small pan and cover with water. Bring to a boil, then simmer gently for 15 minutes. Remove from the heat and set aside.

Heat the oil in a wok and fry the shallots until golden brown and crisp. Remove and set aside. Add the garlic to the wok and stir-fry for a few seconds until golden brown. Stir in the curry paste and cook for a few seconds. Add the coconut milk, stir thoroughly, then add the pork, stirring to ensure each piece is covered with the curry. Add the fish sauce, sugar, *chipo,* and ground roasted peanuts. Stir well and cook for about 5 minutes.

Prepare four serving bowls. Bring a pot of water to a boil, place the noodles in a strainer with a handle and dip into the water for 2–3 seconds to warm through. Drain and divide between the serving bowls. Arrange the quartered egg on top of the noodles. Ladle the curry over the noodles. Top with the fried shallots and cilantro leaves and serve.

Noodles with Chicken, Pork, and Shrimp
RA MEE SIAM

10 ounces dried egg noodles
3 tablespoons oil
1 medium onion, thinly sliced
**2 teaspoons peeled and finely chopped
    fresh ginger**
1 tablespoon Red Curry Paste (see page 28)
2 tablespoons fish sauce
5 ounces chicken breast, thinly sliced
5 ounces boneless pork, thinly sliced
5 ounces raw shrimp, peeled and deveined
1 tablespoon light soy sauce
3 cups bean sprouts
3 scallions, cut into 2-inch lengths
2 limes, cut into wedges, for garnishing

Cook the noodles in boiling water according to the instructions on the package. Drain and rinse under cold water. Tip them into a bowl and mix with 1 tablespoon of the oil.

Heat the remaining oil in a wok and fry the onion and ginger until soft. Add the curry paste, stirring well, then add the fish sauce, chicken, pork, and shrimp. Cook for 2–3 minutes, stirring constantly. Add the noodles, light soy sauce, bean sprouts, and scallions. Stir-fry for 5–6 minutes. Ladle into a large serving dish and serve hot or cold with the lime wedges.

Vegetarian Fried Rice
KHAO PAD JAY

This is a great way to use up day-old rice as it is best made with rice that is a little dry.

2 tablespoons oil
1 medium onion, cut into eighths
1 tablespoon Jungle Curry Paste (see page 30)
2 eggs
4½ cups cooked rice
½ cup peas, fresh or frozen
2 ounces (4–5 cobs) baby corn, sliced diagonally
4 dried Chinese mushrooms, soaked in hot
  water for 20 minutes, then drained and
  squeezed, stems removed, cap sliced
2 tablespoons light soy sauce
1 teaspoon sugar
2 scallions, thinly sliced
2 large fresh red chiles, thinly sliced

Heat the oil in a wok. Add the onion and curry paste and stir-fry briefly. Break in the eggs, stirring well for a few minutes until nearly cooked, then add the rice and the remaining ingredients one at a time, stirring between each addition. Turn into a dish and serve.

Lamb Curry with Rice
KHAO MOK KAEK

Fresh Vegetable Pickles (see page 34) is a great contrasting accompaniment to this rich curry, which is just as frequently made with chicken, instead of lamb.

2 pounds lean lamb, cut into cubes
2½ cups water
4 cardamom pods
10 black or white peppercorns
4 cloves
1 medium onion, sliced
½ teaspoon salt
2¹⁄₃ cups rice, washed and drained
2 teaspoons Curry Powder (see page 32)
2 garlic cloves, crushed
2-inch stick of cinnamon

Place the lamb and water in a large pan with the cardamom pods, peppercorns, cloves, onion and salt. Bring to a boil, then simmer gently until the meat is cooked (3–4 minutes).

Remove the meat and set aside, reserving the stock (strained if you wish) in the pan.

Add the rice, curry powder, garlic, and cinnamon stick to the stock and bring to a boil. Add the meat and stir well. Return to a boil, reduce the heat, and cover with a lid. Simmer for 15–20 minutes. Remove from the heat and serve.

Curry Coconut Rice
KHAO GAREE KAI

Crispy onions are deep-fried slices of onion which can be bought ready-made or just as easily deep-fried at home.

2 tablespoons oil
2 garlic cloves, finely chopped
2 tablespoons Home-style Curry Paste
  (see page 31)
2¹/₃ cups long-grain rice
1 teaspoon ground turmeric
3¼ cups coconut milk
1 teaspoon salt
5 fresh kaffir lime leaves

for the garnish
3 hard-boiled eggs, peeled and quartered
1 small cucumber, thinly sliced
2 large fresh red chiles, thinly sliced
2 tablespoons crispy fried onions

Heat the oil in a large heavy pan. Add the garlic and fry over a low heat until golden brown. Add the curry paste and stir well. Add the rice and turmeric and cook for 2 minutes, stirring well.

Heat the coconut milk in a separate pan until almost boiling. Pour the coconut milk over the rice, stirring constantly, until the mixture comes to a boil. Add the salt and kaffir lime leaves. Cover with a tight-fitting lid, reduce the heat to very low, and simmer for 25 minutes.

Remove the lid, stir well, and pile the rice onto a platter. Garnish with the eggs, cucumber, and chiles, and scatter the fried onion on top.

right
Curry Coconut Rice

Fried Curried Rice with Shrimp
KHAO PAD PONG KARI KUNG

2 tablespoons oil
1 garlic clove, finely chopped
2 small fresh red chiles, finely chopped
8 ounces raw shrimp, peeled and deveined
1 small onion, finely chopped
4½ cups plain cooked rice
2 tablespoons fish sauce
2 tablespoons light soy sauce
1 tablespoon Curry Powder (see page 32)
1 teaspoon sugar
2 scallions, chopped into 2-inch lengths
Cilantro leaves, for garnishing

Heat the oil in a wok or frying pan. Add the garlic and fry until golden. Stir in the chiles and shrimp, cook for a few minutes, then add the onion and cooked rice and stir quickly, cooking for a couple of minutes. Add the remaining ingredients and stir to mix thoroughly. Turn onto a serving dish and garnish with cilantro leaves.

Chicken Fried Rice with Green Curry Paste
KHAO PAD KEOW WAN GAI

If I'm cooking at home, this is my favorite dish to make for myself because it's easy and makes a meal in one.

2 tablespoons oil
1 tablespoon Green Curry Paste (see page 28)
1 skinless chicken breast fillet, cut into small pieces
2 eggs
4 cups cooked rice
1 cup peas, fresh or frozen
2 scallions, finely chopped
1 tablespoon fish sauce
1 tablespoon light soy sauce

Heat the oil in a wok. Add the curry paste and stir-fry for 1 minute, then add the chicken and stir well, cooking for about 2 minutes. Break in the eggs, stir until nearly cooked, then add the remaining ingredients one at a time, stirring between each addition. Serve hot or cold.

Stuffed Curry Mussels
MOK HOY

This is my grandmother's recipe and she used to cook it when we vacationed by the beach in Hua Hin, not far from Bangkok. It looks and tastes wonderful.

left
Stuffed Curry Mussels

2 pounds mussels
1 cup coconut cream (see page 25)
1 tablespoon Red Curry Paste (see page 28)
2 eggs
2 tablespoons fish sauce
1 teaspoon sugar
4 fresh kaffir lime leaves, finely chopped
1 large fresh red chile, thinly sliced lengthways

Discard any open or broken mussels, scrub the shells with a brush, and remove any beards. Soak the mussels in a bowl of cold water for 15 minutes and drain. Separate the mussel shells, discarding the halves without the flesh.

Stir together the coconut cream and curry paste in a bowl. Break in the eggs and stir well. Add the fish sauce, sugar, and kaffir lime leaves, and stir well.

Spread a teaspoonful of stuffing on each mussel and top with sliced red chile. Place the mussels in a steamer over boiling water for 10 minutes. Remove and serve.

POULTRY

Rice Farmers
CHAO NA

When I was an art student, about ten of us went to stay with a classmate whose parents were rice farmers in Ayutthaya, the former capital of Thailand. We went to paint the landscape. The traditional wooden house was elevated on stilts overlooking the fields of golden green rice, swaying in the fresh clean breeze. Water buffalo were cooling off by wallowing in a nearby pond. Under the house lived chickens and ducks, and there was a small kitchen garden devoted to vegetables and herbs for family meals. Fish came from the small ponds dotted around the rice fields. The self-sufficient economy promoted by

His Majesty King Bhumibol, the present king of Thailand, was very evident here: grow what you need to live on, then sell any surplus.

In the morning, before we were up, my friend's mother would cook us a big pot of wonderful chicken curry, made of course with one of her own free-range chickens. We could take the rice and curry out into the fields for lunch, or go back home and eat. She treated us as her own children and we respected her as we would our own mothers—the Thai way.

Spicy Roast Chicken

GAI OB

Why not try this instead of your usual Sunday roast? The curry paste will give it a Thai twist.

3-pound whole chicken
3 tablespoons oil
2 tablespoons Kua Curry Paste (see page 30)
2 tablespoons light soy sauce
2 teaspoons brown sugar
1 tablespoon lime juice

Preheat the oven to 350°F. Use a large cleaver to split the chicken in half down the backbone. Place the chicken, skin-side up, on a rack in a roasting pan and cook for 30 minutes.

Heat the oil in a pan and add the curry paste, stirring well. Add the soy sauce, sugar, and lime juice, stirring constantly until combined.

Brush the sauce over the chicken and bake it for another 30 minutes, or until cooked through. Serve warm or at room temperature.

Chicken Penang

PENANG GAI

This dish is of Malaysian origin and has always been one of the most popular curries in my restaurants in London and America. Now you can make it yourself at home.

2 cups coconut cream (see page 25)
2 tablespoons oil
2 tablespoons Penang Curry Paste (see page 29)
1 pound boneless chicken breast, thinly sliced
3 tablespoons fish sauce
2 teaspoons sugar
4 fresh kaffir lime leaves, finely chopped
2 large fresh red chiles, thinly sliced
20 holy basil leaves

Gently heat the coconut cream in a small pan, but do not let it boil. Remove and set aside, reserving 1 tablespoon as a garnish.

Heat the oil in a wok or pan, add the curry paste, and stir-fry briefly for about 5 minutes. Add the chicken and stir-fry until it is lightly cooked. Stir in the coconut cream, fish sauce, and sugar, stir well for a few minutes, then add the lime leaves, chiles, and basil. Spoon into a bowl and top with the reserved coconut cream.

right
Chicken Penang

Spicy Coconut Chicken
GAI KRATI

Palm sugar, also called jaggery, is made from the sap of the coconut palm and has a rich caramel taste. If you can't find it, use soft brown sugar.

2 tablespoons oil
2 tablespoons Kua Curry Paste (see page 30)
2 cups coconut cream (see page 25)
2 lemongrass stalks, chopped
2 tablespoons fish sauce
1 tablespoon palm sugar (or soft brown sugar)
1/2 teaspoon salt
3½-pound whole chicken, jointed into
  8–10 pieces
4 fresh kaffir lime leaves, finely sliced
2 large fresh red chiles, finely sliced

Heat the oil in a large pan, add the curry paste, and stir well. Add the coconut cream, lemongrass, fish sauce, sugar, and salt, and stir the mixture to combine. Add the chicken pieces and stir until well-coated with the sauce. Bring to a boil, then simmer, uncovered, for 30 minutes or until the chicken is tender.

Ladle into a serving dish and garnish with the kaffir lime leaves and red chiles.

Southern Chicken Curry
GAI KELEK

Kelek is the Thai name for a fishing boat. These boats are brightly painted and the curry reflects their colors. In this dish, butter is used as well as oil, a sign of the Malay Muslim influence.

left
Southern
Chicken Curry

2 tablespoons oil
2 tablespoons butter
3½-pound whole chicken, quartered, then cut
  into small pieces, on the bone
2 tablespoons Kua Curry Paste (see page 30)
2 cups coconut cream (see page 25)
2 cups water
1 tablespoon palm sugar (or soft brown sugar)
3 tablespoons fish sauce
2 zucchinis, thickly sliced
3 tablespoons lime juice
2 large fresh red chiles, finely sliced

Heat the oil and butter in a large pot and fry the chicken pieces until just golden brown. Stir in the curry paste, coconut cream, water, sugar, and fish sauce. Cover and cook over a low heat for 30 minutes or until the chicken is very tender.

Add the zucchini, lime juice, and chiles, cook for another 5–8 minutes and serve.

Chicken and Lime Curry
GAENG GAI MA-NOW

A refreshing dish that is cooked with whole limes as well as kaffir lime leaves.

2 tablespoons oil
2 tablespoons Orange Curry Paste
  (see page 31)
3-pound whole chicken, cut into 8 pieces
1 cup coconut cream (see page 25)
2 limes, cut in half
6 fresh kaffir lime leaves, finely shredded
1 teaspoon salt
1 teaspoon sugar
Cilantro leaves, for garnishing

Heat the oil in a large pan and add the curry paste. Stir over a low heat, then add the chicken and stir-fry for 3–4 minutes, ensuring that the chicken is coated with the paste.

Add the coconut cream, lime halves, shredded kaffir lime leaves, salt, and sugar, then cover and simmer for about 30 minutes or until the chicken is tender. Garnish with the cilantro and serve.

right
Chicken and
Lime Curry

Chicken Curry with Green Banana
GAENG GAI KLOI

Like green papayas, green or unripe bananas are treated like vegetables in Thailand, similar to how plantains are used in African cooking.

4 cups water
4 green bananas, peeled and cut into large
  chunks
1 teaspoon salt
4 chicken legs (thighs and drumsticks)
2 tablespoons oil
1¼-inch piece of fresh ginger, peeled and
  finely chopped
2 tablespoons Orange Curry Paste (see page 31)
1 cup coconut cream (see page 25)
1 cup chicken stock
2 tablespoons fish sauce
2 teaspoons sugar
1 teaspoon salt

Put the water in a large pot, bring to a boil, then add the banana and salt and bring to a boil again. Simmer for 3 minutes, then drain and set aside.

Use the heel of a knife to chop off the thin end of the drumsticks. Chop the thighs in half if large.

Heat the oil in a wok or frying pan. Add the ginger and curry paste and stir well. Add the chicken and cook for 4–5 minutes. Stir in the coconut cream, stock, fish sauce, sugar, and salt, then cover and simmer for 20 minutes. Add the banana, simmer for another 5 minutes, and serve.

Black Pepper Chicken Curry
GAENG GAI PRIK THAI DUM

1 cup coconut cream (see page 25)
2 tablespoons black peppercorns, crushed
2 tablespoons finely chopped ginger,
  ground to a paste
2 tablespoons finely chopped garlic,
  ground to a paste
1/2 teaspoon salt
2 tablespoons finely chopped fresh cilantro
  stems
2 tablespoons lime juice
2 pounds boneless chicken breast, cut into
  1/2-inch cubes

for the curry
3 tablespoons oil
1 large onion, chopped
1 tablespoon Green Curry Paste (see page 28)
1 large tomato, chopped
1 cup water
2 tablespoons fish sauce
1 teaspoon sugar

Mix together the coconut cream, peppercorns, ginger, garlic, salt, cilantro stems, lime juice, and chicken in a non-metallic bowl. Cover and marinate in the fridge for 1 hour.

To make the curry, heat the oil in a wok, fry the onion for about 3 minutes until golden brown, then stir in the curry paste and chopped tomato. Reduce the heat and simmer for 2 minutes.

Add the marinated chicken mixture, together with the water, fish sauce, and sugar. Bring to a boil, stirring, then reduce the heat and simmer for 20 minutes. Serve.

PEPPERCORNS
White peppercorns are picked when young and unripe, and then dried. They have a milder taste than black peppercorns, which are picked when ripe before being dried.

Chicken Curry with Sour Bamboo Shoots
GAENG GAI NORMAI DONG

Here, bamboo shoots counter the sweetness of the palm sugar—see page 152 for more about pickled bamboo shoots.

2 cups coconut cream (see page 25)
2 tablespoons Red Curry Paste (see page 28)
3–4-pound whole chicken, cut into small chunks on the bone
2 cups water
1 pound pickled bamboo shoots
3 tablespoons fish sauce
2 teaspoons palm sugar
5 fresh kaffir lime leaves
2 large fresh red chiles, finely sliced
20 sweet basil leaves

Gently heat the coconut cream in a large pan, stirring well, and simmer for 1 minute. Add the curry paste, stir, then add the chicken pieces and simmer for 15 minutes.

Add the water, bamboo shoots, fish sauce, sugar, and lime leaves. Return to a boil, then simmer for about 20 minutes until the chicken is tender. Add the chiles and basil leaves, and serve.

right
Chicken Curry with Sour Bamboo Shoots

Northern Chicken Curry
GAENG GAI CHIANG RAI

This curry is from Chiang Rai in the north of Thailand and its strong gingery flavor is characteristic of Burmese cooking.

2 tablespoons oil
2 large onions, roughly chopped
3 large garlic cloves, roughly chopped
2-inch piece of ginger, roughly chopped
2 tablespoons Kua Curry Paste (see page 30)
2 pounds boneless chicken thighs, thinly sliced
1/2 teaspoon salt
2 cups coconut milk
2 tablespoons fish sauce
2 teaspoons sugar
2 tablespoons lime juice

Heat the oil in a large pan, add the onion, garlic, and ginger, and stir-fry for a few minutes. Add the curry paste and stir. Add the chicken and cook over a medium heat, turning until golden brown on all sides.

Add the salt and coconut milk. Bring to a boil, then reduce the heat, and stir in the fish sauce and sugar. Simmer, uncovered, for 10 minutes or until the chicken is tender. Just before serving, stir in the lime juice.

Northeastern Steamed Chicken Curry in Banana Leaf
HAW NUNG GAI

Every part of the banana tree is used in Asia. Banana leaves are very useful for wrapping food during steaming and they also impart a subtle flavor to the food. If you can't find them, aluminum foil or small bowls can be used as a substitute in this recipe.

1 pound boneless chicken breasts, cut into small pieces
1 tablespoon Jungle Curry Paste (see page 30)
5 round Thai eggplants, quartered
5 Chinese long beans, cut into 1½-inch lengths
8 ounces dried vermicelli noodles, soaked in cold water for 30 minutes, then drained
3 tablespoons water
4 fresh kaffir lime leaves, finely sliced
2 tablespoons fish sauce
1 teaspoon sugar
5 sprigs of cilantro, finely chopped

6 pieces of banana leaf or aluminum foil, each approximately 8 inches square
Toothpicks

Place all the ingredients in a bowl and mix well. Take 2 tablespoons of the mixture and place on a piece of banana leaf. Fold the leaf around the mixture to form a pyramid, then secure with toothpicks.

Repeat to make six pyramids. Transfer to a steamer and steam for 8 minutes, then serve.

Chicken Massaman Curry
GAENG MASSAMAN GAI

3 tablespoons oil
2 pounds chicken legs
2 tablespoons Massaman Curry Paste
    (see page 29)
2 cups coconut cream (see page 25)
1 pound potatoes, peeled and cut into
    2.5cm cubes
4 small onions, peeled and quartered
4 fresh kaffir lime leaves, roughly torn
2 cups water
3 tablespoons fish sauce
1 tablespoon palm sugar (or soft brown sugar)
2 tablespoons tamarind water (see page 83)
3 tablespoons chopped roasted salted peanuts
2 large fresh red chiles, finely sliced

Heat the oil in a large pan and fry the chicken legs until golden. Remove the chicken and set aside. Reduce the heat and stir in the curry paste, then add the coconut cream and simmer for 2 minutes.

Return the chicken to the pan, simmer for about 10 minutes, then add the potatoes and simmer for another 5 minutes. Add the remaining ingredients, except the chiles, and cook for a final 10 minutes. Add the chiles and serve.

right
Chicken Massaman Curry

Spicy Stuffed Roast Chicken
GAI SOT SAI

3½-pound whole chicken
2 garlic cloves, crushed
1 tablespoon oil
1 tablespoon Red Curry Paste (see page 28)
½ cup coconut milk

for the stuffing
1 tablespoon oil
2 medium onions, chopped
8 ounces ground pork
¾ cup unsalted roasted peanuts, roughly
    chopped
2 teaspoons tamarind water (see page 83)
2 tablespoons chopped fresh cilantro leaves
1 tablespoon chopped fresh mint leaves
1/2 teaspoon salt

Preheat the oven to 350°F. To make the stuffing, heat the oil in a wok, add the onions and cook over a medium heat for 2–3 minutes. Add the pork and cook for 5 minutes or until the meat is brown.

Remove the wok from the heat, and stir in the peanuts, tamarind water, cilantro, mint, and salt. Allow the mixture to cool slightly.

Remove any excess fat from the chicken, rub the skin and inside the cavity with the garlic, then stuff with the pork mixture. Secure the opening with a wooden skewer and tie the legs together with string. Lightly brush the outside of the chicken with the oil, then rub with the curry paste. Place the chicken on a rack in a roasting pan and roast for 20 minutes.

Remove the chicken from the oven, baste it with the coconut milk and cook for another 40 minutes. Remove the skewer and string, and serve.

Tamarind Chicken
GAI MAKHAM

Tamarind water adds a sour, zesty taste to curries and other dishes, but you can use lime juice as a substitute —double the quantity though.

4 chicken drumsticks
4 chicken thighs
2 tablespoons tamarind water (see below)
1 tablespoon Massaman Curry Paste
  (see page 29)
1 teaspoon salt
Oil, for deep-frying
2 scallions, finely chopped, for garnishing

Remove the skin from the chicken pieces. Place the pieces in a large pan and just cover with water. Bring to a boil, then cover the pan and simmer for 10 minutes or until the chicken is cooked through. Drain and cool.

To make the marinade, mix together the tamarind water, curry paste, and salt. Thoroughly coat the cooled chicken, transfer to a non-metallic dish, cover, and let it marinate in the fridge for at least 3 hours.

Heat the oil in a frying pan and cook the chicken over a medium heat until golden brown and heated through. Drain the chicken on paper towels and serve warm, garnished with scallions.

HOW TO MAKE TAMARIND WATER
Take a dried tamarind bundle, put in a bowl, and cover with hot water. Let it soak for about 5 minutes and then use a fork to break up the tamarind, mixing well. Gather up the remaining pulp using your fingers, squeeze well, and discard. (Some village people in Thailand dry-fry the remaining seeds and eat with salt and sugar as a snack, but this is probably an acquired taste!). The tamarind water will keep for a few days in the fridge.

Fried Crispy Pheasant
NOK TOD

This is an Eastern-style dish that can also be cooked with chicken. Serve with sticky rice and papaya salad *(som tam)*—heaven!

2 pheasants, cut into 4 pieces
2 tablespoons Penang Curry Paste (see page 29)
1 teaspoon salt
1 teaspoon sugar
Oil, for deep-frying

Boil the pheasant in a large pot of water for about 10 minutes or until cooked through. Drain and let it cool. Brush the curry paste over the cooled pieces, transfer to a non-metallic dish, and sprinkle with the salt and sugar. Cover and let it marinate in the fridge for 30 minutes.

Heat the oil in a heavy pan, add the pheasant, and cook until golden brown, turning frequently. Drain on kitchen paper. Serve hot or cold.

right
Fried Crispy Pheasant

Barbecued Spicy Quail
NOK PING

In Thailand this dish is cooked with pigeon but I've used quail here as it is more readily available in the West. Once your neighbors smell this cooking, they'll soon be over to join the party!

4 quails
2 tablespoons Penang Curry Paste (see page 29)
4 tablespoons honey
1 tablespoon dark soy sauce
1 tablespoon light soy sauce
Lettuce leaves, for garnishing

8 bamboo skewers

Remove the backbones from the quails by cutting down either side with a pair of kitchen scissors. Flatten the birds with the palm of your hand and secure each one with 2 bamboo skewers.

To make the marinade, mix the curry paste, honey, dark soy sauce and light soy sauce in a small bowl and combine well. Place the quails in a non-metallic dish, pour the marinade over them, and let them marinate in the fridge for at least 3 hours.

Preheat a broiler or barbecue to a medium temperature and cook the quails for about 8–10 minutes on each side. Arrange on the lettuce leaves and serve.

Roast Duck with Lychee Curry
GAENG BET YANG

Lychees are sweet, juicy fruits that contrast wonderfully with the taste and texture of duck.

4-pound whole duck
5 cardamom pods or bay leaves
5 garlic cloves, roughly chopped
1 tablespoon finely chopped cilantro root
1 tablespoon dark soy sauce
1 teaspoon salt
1 teaspoon sugar
1 teaspoon ground white pepper
20 cloves

for the curry
2 cups coconut cream (see page 25)
2 tablespoons Red Curry Paste (see page 28)
3 tablespoons fish sauce
1 teaspoon sugar
5 fresh kaffir lime leaves
1 cup water
20 fresh lychees, pitted, or canned ones, drained
10 cherry tomatoes
20 sweet basil leaves

Clean and dry the duck and place the cardamom or bay leaves inside the cavity. Mix together all the remaining ingredients except the cloves. Spread this mixture over the duck and press the cloves into the skin. Transfer the duck to a non-metallic dish, cover, and marinate in the fridge for at least 3 hours.

Preheat the oven to 425°F. Roast the duck for 20 minutes, then reduce the heat to 350°F and cook for another 2 hours. Remove from the oven, let it cool, then shred the meat from the bird.

To make the curry, gently heat the coconut cream in a large pan. Simmer for 2 minutes, then stir in the curry paste, fish sauce, sugar, and kaffir lime leaves. Simmer for 2 minutes, then add the duck meat. Bring to a boil, slowly pour in the water, and simmer for 10 minutes.

Add the lychees and tomatoes and simmer for another 5 minutes. Add the basil leaves and serve.

Hot Duck Curry
GAENG PET BET

This is more like an Indian curry because there are no vegetables in it at all, just a little meat. Serve with Fresh Vegetable Pickles (*Ajart*)—see page 34.

6-pound whole duck
5 cups water
6 fresh kaffir lime leaves
1 teaspoon salt
2 tablespoons oil
2 tablespoons Red Curry Paste (see page 28)
1 cup coconut milk
1 tablespoon sugar
2 tablespoons lime juice
Small bunch of cilantro, chopped, for garnishing

To portion the duck, first remove the legs. Separate the thighs from the drumsticks and chop each thigh and drumstick into 2. Trim away the lower half of the duck carcass with kitchen scissors. Cut the breast piece in half down the middle, then chop each half into 4.

Place the duck meat and bones into a large pot and cover with the water. Add the kaffir lime leaves and 1/2 teaspoon of salt, bring to a boil and simmer, uncovered, for 30 minutes or until the meat is tender. Discard the bones, skim off the fat from the stock, and set aside.

Heat the oil in a frying pan, add the curry paste and stir well. Add the coconut milk, sugar, remaining salt, and lime juice, and simmer briefly.

Stir the curry paste mixture into the pot with the duck and stock, bring to a boil and simmer, uncovered, for 20 minutes. Ladle into a serving dish and garnish with cilantro.

Crispy Duck with Curry Sauce
PET GROB

You need to prepare this dish in advance to ensure the duck is really crispy.

4–5-pound whole duck
2 teaspoons salt
5 star anise
1 tablespoon Szechuan peppercorns
2 cinnamon sticks
1 teaspoon cloves
4 slices of fresh ginger
5 tablespoons rice wine or dry sherry
Oil, for deep-frying

for the curry sauce
2 tablespoons oil
2 tablespoons Red Curry Paste (see page 28)
2 cups coconut cream (see page 25)
12 ounces new potatoes, peeled and cut into
  1-inch cubes
10 ounces carrots, peeled and cut into
  1-inch cubes
2 cups water
2 tablespoons tamarind water (see page 83)
2 teaspoons sugar
2 teaspoons salt
5 fresh kaffir lime leaves, finely chopped

Remove the wing tips from the duck and discard. Use a large cleaver to split the bird in half down the backbone. Rub salt all over both halves. Place the duck in a non-metallic dish with the spices, ginger, and rice wine, then cover and let it marinate in the fridge for 4 hours.

Remove the duck from the marinade, transfer to a steamer, and vigorously steam the duck with the marinade for 3 hours, topping up the boiling water as necessary.

Remove the duck and let cool for at least 5 hours— the duck must be completely cold and dry or the skin will not be crispy.

To make the curry sauce, heat the oil in a wok, add the curry paste, and stir well. Add the coconut cream, potatoes, and carrots, and stir-fry for about 2 minutes. Add the water, tamarind water, sugar, salt, and kaffir lime leaves, and bring to a boil. Cover the wok and cook until the potatoes are soft.

To finish the duck, heat the oil in another wok or large pan. Place the duck halves in the oil, skin-side down, and deep-fry for 5–6 minutes or until crisp and brown, turning just once at the very last moment. Remove, drain on paper towels, and serve with the curry sauce.

Duck Curry
BET KARI

2 tablespoons oil
2 tablespoons butter
5 cardamom seeds
2-inch stick of cinnamon
5 cloves
2 tablespoons finely chopped shallot
2 tablespoons finely chopped ginger
3 tablespoons finely chopped garlic
1½ pounds boneless duck thighs, cut into
**   1¼-inch cubes**
2 cups coconut milk
2 teaspoons salt
2 teaspoons sugar
1 medium potato, peeled and cut into
**   1-inch cubes**
2 tablespoons Curry Powder (see page 32)
1 teaspoon ground white pepper
2 medium onions, roughly chopped
1 large fresh red chile, finely sliced
1 large fresh green chile, finely sliced
2 tomatoes, quartered
Cilantro leaves, for garnishing

Heat the oil and the butter in a large pan. Add the cardamom, cinnamon, and cloves, and cook over a medium heat for about 1 minute.

Add the shallot, ginger, and garlic, and stir well. Add the duck and fry until golden brown on all sides. Stir in the coconut milk, salt, sugar, and potato, and cook for 10 minutes, then add the curry powder, pepper, and onions. Cover and simmer for 15 minutes.

Add the chiles and tomatoes and cook for another 5 minutes. Garnish with cilantro and serve.

Roasted Duck with Green Curry Paste
BET KEOW WAN

6 duck thighs
2 tablespoons Green Curry Paste (see page 28)
½ teaspoon salt
2 teaspoons palm sugar (or soft brown sugar)
2 tablespoons fish sauce

Trim off any excess fat from the duck. Cut a few slits in each thigh.

Mix together the curry paste, salt, palm sugar, and fish sauce. Place the duck in a shallow non-metallic dish and rub it all over with the mixture. Cover and let it marinate in the fridge for at least 3 hours.

Preheat the oven to 350°F. Roast the duck for 45 minutes. Serve hot or cold.

MEAT

Village Market
CHAO BHAN

Village farmers make a living by growing rice that they sell to factories. The rest of their land is used to grow herbs and vegetables, and usually cows or pigs are kept, too. These provide food for the family and any surplus is sold at farmer's markets for extra income. At the market, the meat stalls are a riot of color. Strings of sausages, which may be fresh or fermented, smoked or unsmoked, hang from the rafters along with bags of fried pork rinds and other delicacies. Metal trays display cuts of fresh meat alongside glistening organ meats, and, in the north, they may be accompanied by a few pigs' heads. In Isaan province, shoppers may come across insects—beetles, larvae, grasshoppers, and even scorpions!

In the past, Thais did not eat a great deal of meat, partly because of the influence of Buddhism and its non-violent teachings, and partly because of scarce resources. The eating of meat was largely reserved for religious festivals and other special occasions. Large animals, such as water buffalo which were considered sacred, were only slaughtered for the pot if they were injured. But today, as a result of greater affluence and improved transport, meat is a much more important part of the diet in Thailand than it used to be. Nevertheless, Thais do not eat a great deal of meat by Western standards and the portions tend to be smaller.

Pork in Red Curry with Pumpkin
GAENG PET MOO FAENGTONG

This is a classic Thai curry that combines meat and vegetables, in this case pumpkin. Any kind of pumpkin or squash will work in this dish.

2 tablespoons oil
2 tablespoons Red Curry Paste (see page 28)
2 pounds boneless pork, cut into thick strips
2 cups coconut milk
2 cups water
1 pound pumpkin, peeled and cut into
small cubes
6 fresh kaffir lime leaves
3 tablespoons fish sauce
1 teaspoon sugar
2 large fresh green chiles, thinly sliced
10 basil leaves, for garnishing

Heat the oil in a wok, add the curry paste, and stir. Add the meat and stir-fry until golden brown. Stir in the coconut milk, then add the water and simmer for 15 minutes.

Add the pumpkin, lime leaves, fish sauce, and sugar. Reduce the heat and simmer for another 15 minutes. Add the chiles, stir once, then ladle into a serving dish and garnish with the basil.

Pork Curry with Pickled Garlic
GAENG HUNG LAY

This is a specialty of northern Thailand.

2 tablespoons oil
2 garlic cloves, finely chopped
2 tablespoons Kua Curry Paste (see page 30)
2 pounds boneless pork with a little fat, cut into
 1-inch cubes
2 cups coconut cream (see page 25)
2 cups stock or water
2-inch piece of fresh ginger, peeled and
 finely chopped
3 tablespoons fish sauce
2 teaspoons sugar
4 whole heads of Pickled Garlic, finely sliced
 (see page 34)

Heat the oil in a wok, add the chopped garlic, and fry until golden brown. Add the curry paste and stir well. Add the pork and stir-fry for around 5 minutes or until cooked through.

Pour in the coconut cream and stir until it begins to reduce and thicken, then pour in the stock. Simmer gently for 10 minutes, then stir in the ginger, fish sauce, sugar, and pickled garlic. Ladle into a large bowl and serve.

PICKLED GARLIC
You can use store-bought pickled garlic or make your own as shown on page 34. Garlic can either be pickled in whole heads as seen on the right or separated into individual cloves before pickling.

Pork Penang Curry
MOO PENANG

This is quite a mild and not-too spicy curry and I sometimes eat it for breakfast with bread.

2 tablespoons oil
2 tablespoons Penang Curry Paste (see page 29)
2 pounds boneless pork tenderloin, cut into
  thin strips
2 cups coconut milk
3 tablespoons fish sauce
2 teaspoons sugar
20 sweet basil leaves
1 large fresh red chile, thinly sliced,
  for garnishing

Heat the oil in a wok, add the curry paste, and stir well. Add the pork and stir-fry for 5–10 minutes until tender and light brown. Add the coconut milk, fish sauce, and sugar, and simmer, uncovered, for 2–3 minutes.

Add the basil leaves. Stir briefly and ladle into a serving dish. Garnish with the sliced chile and serve.

Fried Pork Curry
PAT PET MOO

Bamboo shoots are available in cans from the supermarket (see page 152). Once opened, keep the contents in fresh water in a sealed jar for up to a week in the fridge.

3 tablespoons oil
2 tablespoons Orange Curry Paste (see page 31)
2 pounds boneless pork, cut into 1¼-inch cubes
3 tablespoons fish sauce
2 teaspoons sugar
1 cup water
6 ounces bamboo shoots, thinly sliced
1 large fresh red chile, finely sliced
1 large fresh green chile, finely sliced
20 holy basil leaves

Heat the oil in a large pan, add the curry paste, and stir. Add the pork and stir until the meat is well coated with the curry paste. Add the fish sauce, sugar, and water, cover, and simmer gently for 45 minutes or until the meat is tender.

Add the bamboo shoots and chiles, stirring well, then add the basil just before serving.

Roast Spicy Pork Chops
GADOOK MOO YANG

I've adapted this dish for Western tastes by keeping the pork chops whole. Traditionally, the meat would be sliced and shared around.

left
Roast Spicy
Pork Chops

2 tablespoons oil
2 tablespoons light soy sauce
2 tablespoons Penang Curry Paste (see page 29)
2 tablespoons honey
¹/₂ teaspoon salt
3 pounds pork chops
2 limes, cut into wedges, for serving

Combine the oil, soy sauce, curry paste, honey, and salt in a large bowl. Add the pork chops and stir until the chops are completely coated in the marinade. Cover and let marinate in the fridge for at least 3 hours.

Preheat the oven to 350°F. Place the chops in an oiled baking dish and cook for 50 minutes. Garnish with the lime wedges and serve.

Pork Red Curry
GAENG DAENG MOO

One of my aunts gave me this recipe. Thai people like to eat at home and there is always something special to try in the homes of friends and family.

2 tablespoons Red Curry Paste (see page 28)
1 pound pork tenderloin, sliced into medallions
2 tablespoons tamarind water (see page 83)
2 tablespoons oil
1 cup coconut milk
2 tablespoons fish sauce
2 teaspoons sugar
2 large dried red chiles, roughly chopped

Mix together the curry paste, pork, and tamarind water, and place in a shallow, non-metallic dish. Cover and let marinate in the fridge for 1 hour.

Heat the oil in a wok, add the marinated pork, and cook over a high heat for 5 minutes, stirring. Add the coconut milk, stir, and simmer for 5 minutes. Stir in the fish sauce, sugar, and dried red chiles, and serve.

Stir-fried Ground Pork with Eggplant and Green Curry Paste
MOO PAD MAKUA

If you cannot find round Thai eggplants, you can substitute the common purple-black variety.

2 tablespoons oil
1 tablespoon Green Curry Paste (see page 28)
8 ounces ground pork
2 long Thai eggplants, thickly sliced
2 tablespoons bean sauce (see page 25)
1 tablespoon light soy sauce
1 teaspoon sugar
20 sweet basil leaves
1 large fresh red chile, finely sliced

Heat the oil in a wok, add the curry paste, and stir well. Stir in the pork, then add the eggplant and stir again, cooking for about 8 minutes. Add the bean sauce, soy sauce, and sugar, then stir-fry for about 3 minutes (cover the pan with a lid or foil and the steam will help it cook faster).

Add the basil and chile, stir thoroughly, then ladle into a dish and serve.

Spicy Pork with Long Beans
MOO PAD PRIK KING

Make sure you cook the beans very briefly—they should be slightly crunchy rather than soft. See page 156 for more on long beans.

See page 156

left
**Spicy Pork with
Long Beans**

**2 tablespoons oil
1 tablespoon Red Curry Paste (see page 28)
8 ounces boneless pork, finely sliced
8 ounces long beans, chopped into 1-inch pieces
2 tablespoons fish sauce
1 teaspoon sugar
1 tablespoon ground roasted peanuts
4 fresh kaffir lime leaves, finely chopped**

Heat the oil in a wok, add the curry paste, and stir well. Add the pork and stir-fry until just cooked, then add the long beans, fish sauce, sugar, peanuts, and kaffir lime leaves. Stir-fry until the beans are just cooked, then serve on a platter, with noodles, if you like.

Spicy Spare Ribs
KUA HAENG SI KRONG MOO

This is a very quick and easy dish to cook. Use young spare ribs if you can get them.

**3 tablespoons oil
2 pounds spare ribs, chopped into
    1¼-inch pieces
1 tablespoon Kua Curry Paste (see page 30)
½ cup coconut cream (see page 25)
2 tablespoons fish sauce
1 teaspoon palm sugar (or soft brown sugar)
5 fresh kaffir lime leaves, finely sliced**

Heat the oil in a wok and fry the ribs for 5–10 minutes until cooked through and golden brown on all sides. Add the curry paste, stir, and very slowly add the coconut cream along with the remaining ingredients, stirring gently all the time. Bring to a boil and simmer for a few minutes. Ladle into a dish and serve.

Spare Rib Curry with Bitter Melon
GAENG MARAK

Bitter melon is pear shaped with a green warty skin, and is in fact an immature melon. It is sometimes compared to cucumbers but has the bitterness of Belgian endive leaves. It can be found in most Chinese supermarkets. Use young spare ribs if you can get them because the meat is more tender.

2 tablespoons oil
2 tablespoons Kua Curry Paste (see page 30)
5½ cups water
2 lemongrass stalks, cut into 2-inch lengths
5 fresh kaffir lime leaves
3 tablespoons fish sauce
1 teaspoon salt
2 teaspoons sugar
1½ pounds spare ribs, chopped into
   1¼-inch pieces
2 bitter melons, cut in half lengthways, then
   sliced into wedges about 1¼ inches wide
2 scallions, roughly chopped
3 cilantro sprigs, finely chopped, for garnishing

Heat the oil in a wok, add the curry paste, and stir well. Add the water, lemongrass, kaffir lime leaves, fish sauce, salt, and sugar, then bring to a boil. Add the spare ribs, reduce the heat, and simmer for 10–15 minutes.

Add the bitter melon and cook gently for another 4–5 minutes, then add the scallions. Garnish with cilantro and serve.

Northern Mixed Meat Curry
GAENG HOH

The idea behind this dish is that it uses up leftovers. Whatever remains from yesterday's dinner—curry, noodles, fried vegetables—all are combined using this method to make a new dish. "Hoh" is northern dialect for "throw" —it's all thrown together!

left
Northern Mixed Meat Curry

3 tablespoons oil
2 tablespoons Red Curry Paste (see page 28)
8 ounces boneless pork, cut into thin strips
8 ounces beef steak, cut into thin strips
½ cup water
4 ounces round Thai eggplants, quartered
4 ounces long beans, cut into 1¼-inch pieces
4 ounces bamboo shoots, thinly sliced
3 tablespoons fish sauce
1 teaspoon sugar
8 ounces vermicelli bean (also called vermicelli cellophane), soaked in cold water for 30 minutes, then drained
2 large fresh red chiles, finely sliced
20 sweet basil leaves, for garnishing

Heat the oil in a wok, add the curry paste, and stir. Add the meat and water, bring to a boil, then simmer for 10 minutes.

Add the remaining ingredients one at a time, and stir-fry, mixing well, for 3 minutes. Ladle into a dish and serve garnished with the basil leaves.

Wild Boar Curry
GAENG BHAN MOO PA

Wild pig is not unusual in Thailand and more or less any cut can be used. Its meat is more chewy than normal pork and the skin is nice and crunchy. Wild boar will work just as well, but if it is not available, farmed pork can be substituted.

1 cup water
1 pound boneless pork, thinly sliced

for the curry
2 tablespoons oil
2 tablespoons Home-style Curry Paste (see page 31)
4 cups water
6 round Thai eggplants, quartered
10 long beans, cut into 1¼-inch lengths
5 ounces bamboo shoots
5 fresh kaffir lime leaves
1 tablespoon finely sliced *krachai* (see page 23)
2 large fresh red chiles, finely sliced
20 basil leaves

Bring the cup of water to a boil in a large pan, add the pork and simmer slowly until tender. Remove the meat from the water and set aside.

Heat the oil in a wok, add the curry paste and stir, then add the meat and stir-fry, ensuring it is coated in the paste. Add the remaining ingredients, except the chiles and basil, then stir and simmer for 10 minutes. Add the chiles and basil, and serve.

Dry Beef Curry
GAENG NUA YALA

The only liquid in this curry is the small amount of stock so it is known as a dry curry. It's from Yala, in the south of Thailand. Curry doesn't have to be served with rice, it's good with noodles, too.

2 tablespoons oil
3 medium onions, sliced
1 tablespoon grated ginger
3 garlic cloves, crushed
1 cinnamon stick
2 tablespoons Massaman Curry Paste
  (see page 29)
2 pounds blade or skirt steak, cut into
  small chunks
½ cup beef stock
1 tablespoon tamarind water (see page 83)
1 teaspoon sugar
½ teaspoon salt

Heat the oil in a large pan, add the onions, ginger, garlic, and cinnamon, and stir over a low heat until the onion is soft.

Add the curry paste and meat, stirring to ensure the meat is well coated. Add the stock, tamarind water, sugar, and salt, then cover and cook over a low heat for 1 hour or until the meat is tender. Remove the cinnamon stick before serving. Serve with noodles or rice.

right
Dry Beef Curry

Beef Curry from Pattani
GAENG NUA PATTANI

I first ate this dish many years ago when visiting an aunt in Pattani in the south of Thailand.

3 tablespoons oil
2 tablespoons Massaman Curry Paste
  (see page 29)
2 pounds chuck steak, cut evenly into
  1¼-inch cubes
2 cups water
1 pound carrots, cut into 1-inch chunks
2 medium onions, cut into eighths
2 teaspoons salt
1 teaspoon ground turmeric
1 teaspoon ground white pepper
2 tablespoons tamarind water (see page 83)

Heat the oil in a large pan, add the curry paste, and stir well. Add the meat and stir-fry until tender, then pour in the water and simmer over a gentle heat for 20 minutes.

Add the remaining ingredients one at a time, and cook for another 15 minutes, then serve.

Grilled Beef Curry with Figs
GAENG MADUA NUA YANG

In Thailand this curry is made with a fruit that looks and tastes similar to a fig but is a bit smaller. I haven't been able to find it in the West so I've adapted this recipe to incorporate figs instead. I always try and reinvent curries using local ingredients.

left
Grilled Beef Curry with Figs

2 cups coconut cream (see page 25)
2 tablespoons Home-style Curry Paste (see page 31)
1 pound tender beef fillet, grilled, then cut into thick slices
8 ounces fresh figs, quartered
1 tablespoon finely sliced _krachai_ (see page 23)
3 tablespoons fish sauce
1 teaspoon sugar
6 fresh kaffir lime leaves
2 cups water
2 large fresh red chiles, finely sliced

Heat the coconut cream in a large pan, stirring constantly for 2 minutes, then add the curry paste and stir for another 2 minutes. Add the remaining ingredients, except the chile, one at a time. Bring to a boil and simmer for 3 minutes. Add the chiles, stir again, and serve.

Hot Dry Beef Curry
NUA KUA KLINK

This curry is a specialty of southern Thailand and is normally eaten very spicy hot.

2 tablespoons oil
1 large onion, finely sliced
2 tablespoons Kua Curry Paste (see page 30)
1 teaspoon salt
1 teaspoon sugar
2 pounds beef round steak, cut into 1¼-inch cubes
4 fresh kaffir lime leaves, roughly chopped
4 small fresh red chiles, finely chopped
1 large tomato, finely chopped, for garnishing

Heat the oil in a large pan, add the onion, and fry until soft. Stir in the curry paste, salt, and sugar. Add the beef and stir well over a medium heat to seal and evenly brown the pieces.

Add the kaffir lime leaves and chiles and continue to stir until the oil separates from the sauce. Cover and cook for about 20 minutes. Garnish with chopped tomato and serve.

Lamb and Okra Curry
GAENG KACHIAP KAEK

It's quite unusual to find curries made with okra in Thailand—this one has an Indian influence.

3 tablespoons oil
2 tablespoons Kua Curry Paste (see page 30)
2 pounds lean lamb, cut into 1-inch cubes
4 tablespoons water
8 ounces okra, washed, trimmed but left whole
2 tablespoons fish sauce
2 teaspoons sugar
Cilantro leaves, chopped, for garnishing

Heat the oil in a frying pan, add the curry paste, and stir well. Add the lamb, stirring to coat. Add the water and stir well. Cover and cook over a low heat for 15–20 minutes until the lamb is tender.

Add the okra, fish sauce, and sugar, and cook over a high heat for about 3 minutes. Garnish with the cilantro and serve.

right
Lamb and Okra Curry

Green Curry with Beef
GAENG KEOW WAN NUA

Everybody in my family loves this curry, and what's more, we can all cook it, too!

3 tablespoons oil
2 tablespoons Green Curry Paste (see page 28)
2 pounds tender beef steak, finely sliced
2 cups coconut cream (see page 25)
2 cups vegetable stock or water
2 large fresh red chiles, sliced diagonally into
   thin ovals
3 tablespoons fish sauce
12 round Thai eggplants, quartered
1 tablespoon sugar
40 sweet basil leaves

Heat the oil in a large pan and add the curry paste, stirring well. Add the beef and stir-fry until just cooked. Add the coconut cream and stir constantly as it comes to a boil.

Add the stock, return to a boil, stirring constantly. Add the chiles, fish sauce, eggplants, and sugar, and simmer until the eggplants are cooked. Stir in the basil leaves just before serving.

Massaman Lamb Curry
MASSAMAN KAEK

All my Western friends love this one. It's spicy but doesn't have too much chile. You can eat it with bread, Indian style. The name Massaman comes from the Thai word for Muslim.

left
Massaman
Lamb Curry

2 cups coconut cream (see page 25)
2 tablespoons oil
2 tablespoons Massaman Curry Paste
  (see page 29)
2 pounds lamb, cut into 1¼-inch cubes
2 tablespoons tamarind water (see page 83)
2 teaspoons sugar
3 tablespoons fish sauce
2 cups stock or water
6 small potatoes, quartered
4 tablespoons whole roasted peanuts
6 small shallots

Gently warm the coconut cream in a small pan until it just starts to separate. Remove from the heat and set aside.

Heat the oil in a wok, add the curry paste, and stir well. Add half the warmed coconut cream and cook for 2–3 minutes, stirring all the time. Add the lamb and stir to coat in the curry sauce. Add the tamarind water, sugar, fish sauce, and the remaining coconut cream, stirring constantly. Add half the stock, simmer gently for 10 minutes, stirring well, then add the remaining stock and simmer for another 10 minutes, stirring occasionally.

Add the potatoes and simmer for 5 minutes. Add the peanuts and cook for another 5 minutes, then finally stir in the shallots and cook for 5 minutes more. Ladle into a large dish and serve.

Northern Barbecued Thai-meatloaf Patty
AB ONG NUA

1 tablespoon Kua Curry Paste (see page 30)
1 pound ground beef
1 egg
1 tablespoon soy sauce
1 tablespoon fish sauce
1 teaspoon sugar
3 fresh kaffir lime leaves, finely sliced
4 stems of cilantro, finely chopped

1 banana leaf for wrapping (or use
  aluminum foil)
Toothpicks

Place all the ingredients in a large bowl and mix well. Wet your hands and form the mixture into a large patty and place in the center of the banana leaf.

Fold the leaf around the patty and secure with toothpicks. Cook over a hot barbecue for 20 minutes, turning regularly, then serve.

FISH

Fishermen
CHAO PRAMONG

My life now revolves around my restaurants in Miami (Florida) and Ko Samui (Thailand)—both coastal locations where seafood is fresh and easily available. The southern provinces of Thailand all have long coastlines where seafood is plentiful, and which contribute greatly to the local economy and diet.

I recently visited an old school friend, whose family have a deep-sea fishing business based in Chumphon in the south of Thailand. I went to see the boats when they came into port, and was curious about how they worked. My friend explained to me that his boats went out for anywhere up to six days, depending upon how long it took to fill the hold with fish. Each boat has a crew of around 20, including the cooks. I tried to imagine what it would be like to be out on the ocean for almost a week, with nothing to look at but the sea and the sky—no television, no shops, no distractions at all, only the company of the crew, who all live together in a very small space. The cooks have to plan and organize enough food for a week at a time, because of course they have to take everything with them: rice, vegetables, sauces, spices, meat, and chicken. Big pots of curry are the easiest food to prepare and are the main dishes to accompany the rice. Maybe one day I'll become a chef on one of the big cruise ships from Miami to the Bahamas!

Southern Thai Fish Curry
GAENG PET PLA

2 tablespoons oil
2 tablespoons Red Curry Paste (see page 28)
2 cups coconut milk
2 cups fish or vegetable stock, or water
1/2 teaspoon ground turmeric
3 tablespoons fish sauce
1 tablespoon sugar
1 tablespoon tamarind water (see page 83)
1 pound monkfish, hoki or red snapper fillet,
  cut into large chunks
3 tomatoes, quartered
1 red pepper, cored, seeded, and chopped
1 green pepper, cored, seeded, and chopped
Few cilantro leaves, for garnishing

Heat the oil in a large wok, add the curry paste, and stir well. Stir in the coconut milk, stock or water, turmeric, fish sauce, sugar, and tamarind water, and simmer for 5 minutes.

Add the fish and simmer for 6–8 minutes. Stir in the tomatoes and peppers, simmer over a low heat for about 10 minutes until thickened. Ladle into a serving bowl and garnish with cilantro.

right
**Southern Thai
Fish Curry**

Broiled Curried Fish
PLA YANG PRIK GAENG

In this recipe the curry paste is used as a marinade. If you come to my restaurant, Cinnamon Kitchen in Ko Samui, be sure to order this dish!

2 tablespoons oil, plus extra for brushing
1 tablespoon Kua Curry Paste (see page 30)
1 tablespoon fish sauce
1 tablespoon light soy sauce
1 teaspoon sugar
2 tablespoons water
2 trout or red snapper, weighing about
  10 ounces each, cleaned and trimmed
Banana leaf (or tin foil)

for the garnish
Tomato slices
Onion rings
Cucumber slices
Lemon or lime slices
Cilantro sprigs

Heat the oil in a pan, add the curry paste, and stir well. Add the fish sauce, soy sauce, sugar, and water, and cook for 2 minutes, stirring well. Set aside.

Use the point of a sharp knife to make 3 deep cuts along each side of the fish. Spread the marinade over the fish, working it into the cuts. Place in a shallow, non-metallic dish, cover, and let it marinate in the fridge for 3 hours.

Preheat the broiler. Brush the broiler rack with oil. Place the fish on the banana leaf or tin foil and sprinkle a little oil over it. Wrap well and broil for about 7 minutes on each side. Serve garnished with the salad, lemon slices, and cilantro.

Haddock with Green Curry Sauce
KEOW WAN PLA

left
**Haddock with Green
Curry Sauce**

2 cups coconut cream (see page 25)
1 teaspoon salt
2 tablespoons Green Curry Paste (see page 28)
1 tablespoon palm sugar (or soft brown sugar)
4 haddock fillets, each weighing about 6 ounces
10 fresh kaffir lime leaves, finely sliced
2 large fresh red chiles, sliced into thin ovals

Gently heat the coconut cream in a large frying pan, add the salt and stir in the green curry paste, mixing well. Add the palm sugar, stirring constantly. Add the haddock and kaffir lime leaves, then bring slowly to simmering point.

Reduce the heat, cover, and poach the fish for 10–15 minutes, depending on its thickness. Transfer the fish to warmed plates, garnish with chiles, and serve.

Fish Curry with Kaffir Lime
GAENG PLA MAKRUT

For this recipe you will not need all the curry paste you make—there will be enough left over to make three or four more curries.

2 cups coconut milk
2 tablespoons curry paste (see below)
1 teaspoon salt
1 tablespoon palm sugar (or soft brown sugar)
**2 pounds firm white fish fillets, cut into
   1¼-inch chunks**
6 fresh kaffir lime leaves, roughly torn
2 large fresh red chiles, diagonally sliced

for the curry paste
5 dried and 5 fresh red chiles
1/2 teaspoon salt
1 tablespoon black peppercorns
2 tablespoons finely chopped fresh galangal
4 tablespoons finely chopped lemongrass
2 teaspoons grated kaffir lime peel
**2 teaspoons finely chopped fresh turmeric (if
   unavailable, use the same quantity of ground)**
1 teaspoon shrimp paste

To make the paste, pound each of the ingredients, one at a time, in a mortar, until a paste is formed.

To make the curry, gently warm the coconut milk in a pan, then add the curry paste, salt, and sugar. Bring to a boil, add the fish and kaffir lime leaves, bring back to a boil, and simmer for about 3 minutes, stirring gently. Add the chiles and serve.

Mackerel in Red Curry
CHU CHEE PLA

Mackerel is a popular fish in Thailand and this is a simple and satisfying curry.

4 tablespoons oil
3 mackerel fillets, cleaned
1 tablespoon Red Curry Paste (see page 28)
1 cup coconut cream (see page 25)
2 tablespoons fish sauce
1 teaspoon sugar
5 fresh kaffir lime leaves, finely sliced
2 large fresh red chiles, thinly sliced
20 sweet basil leaves

Heat 2 tablespoons of oil in a large, deep-sided frying pan, add the mackerel and fry over a medium heat for 5–7 minutes or until the fish is cooked. Remove the fish from the oil, drain on paper towels, and set aside.

Heat the remaining oil in the frying pan, add the curry paste, and stir well, then add the coconut cream and the remaining ingredients. Add the fish to the pan and cook for another 2–3 minutes, stirring constantly. Ladle into a dish, add the basil leaves, and serve.

right
**Mackerel in
Red Curry**

Barbecued Curried Squid
PLA MUK KORLEH

This is a mild dish, suitable for those who are not keen on hot food! It's the perfect streetfood to eat on the beach with a beer. The sellers have portable charcoal barbecues to cook the squid on.

2 cups coconut milk
2 tablespoons Curry Powder (see page 32)
1 teaspoon salt
1 teaspoon sugar
1 teaspoon ground white pepper
2 tablespoons tamarind water (see page 83)
2 pounds large squid, cleaned

Heat the coconut milk, curry powder, salt, sugar, white pepper, and tamarind water in a large pan, stirring to mix well. When the sugar has dissolved, remove from the heat and add the squid. Let it marinate for at least 1 hour in the fridge.

Remove the squid from the marinade and place on a preheated barbecue. Cook for 5 minutes on each side, brushing with the marinade. Cut into small pieces to serve.

Fish Curry with Papaya
PLA GAENG SOM

The best papayas to use for this curry are green, unripe ones that are just starting to turn yellow.

left
Fish Curry
with Papaya

4½ cups water
2 tablespoons Orange Curry Paste (see page 31)
1 pound monkfish fillet, cut into large chunks
1 small unripe papaya, peeled, seeded, and
roughly sliced
1 teaspoon salt
2 tablespoons fish sauce
1 tablespoon palm sugar (or soft brown sugar)
3 tablespoons tamarind water (see page 83)
Cilantro leaves and slices of red chile,
for garnishing

Bring the water to a boil in a large pan, add the curry paste, and stir well. Add the fish and cook gently for about 5 minutes.

Add the remaining ingredients, stir well, and gently cook for another 5 minutes. Serve hot, garnished with cilantro and red chile.

Sea Bass with Curry Sauce
PLA LAD PRIK

One of my favorites, so good I never want to share it!

2¼-pound sea bass, cleaned and scaled
1 teaspoon salt
2 tablespoons flour
Oil, for deep-frying

for the curry sauce
2 tablespoons oil
2 tablespoons Home-style Curry Paste
(see page 31)
2 tablespoons fish sauce
2 tablespoons water
1 tablespoon light soy sauce
1 large fresh red chile, thinly sliced
1 large fresh green chile, thinly sliced
2 teaspoons sugar
Cilantro leaves, for garnishing

Use the point of a sharp knife to score both sides of the fish, making diagonal cuts right down to the bone at intervals of about an inch. Rub the whole fish with salt, inside and outside, then coat it from head to tail with flour.

Heat the oil in a wok. Deep-fry the fish in the hot oil for about 4–5 minutes on each side, or until golden brown. Remove the fish, drain on paper towels, then place on a warmed platter.

To make the sauce, heat the oil in a pan, add the curry paste, and stir. Add the fish sauce, water, soy sauce, chiles, and sugar, stirring well until the sauce is smooth and thickened. Pour the curry sauce over the fish and garnish with fresh cilantro.

Curried Fish Balls with Bamboo Shoots
GAENG PA LUKCHIN PLA

Fish balls are like small round dumplings and are made from fish and flour. They can be bought ready prepared in Chinese stores.

2 tablespoons oil
2 tablespoons Jungle Curry Paste (see page 30)
1 pound fish balls
3 cups water
3 tablespoons fish sauce
6 fresh kaffir lime leaves
5 ounces bamboo shoots
1 tablespoon finely sliced *krachai* (see page 23)
20 sweet basil leaves

Heat the oil in a large pan, add the curry paste, then add the fish balls quickly and stir-fry for 2 minutes. Add the remaining ingredients one at a time, stirring well, then bring to a boil. Ladle into a dish, add the basil leaves, and serve.

MAKING FISH BALLS
The skin is removed from the fish and the flesh cut into small pieces. It is then pounded, mixed with a little flour, and molded into fish balls. The fish skin is not discarded—it is sun-dried or deep-fried to crispen and added to curry or noodle soup, or served as a side dish with chili dip (*nam prik*).

Stir-fried Spicy Seafood
PAD PET TALAY

Being Thai, naturally I think this is the best way in the world to cook seafood!

left
Stir-fried
Spicy Seafood

3 tablespoons oil
2 medium onions, sliced
1 tablespoon Red Curry Paste (see page 28)
1 pound raw shrimp, peeled and deveined,
   tails on
6 ounces squid, cut into 2½-inch squares,
   and scored in a criss-cross fashion with a
   small knife
8 ounces mussels, cleaned and debearded
   (discard any with open or broken shells)
1 large tomato, finely chopped
20 basil leaves
2 tablespoons fish sauce
1 teaspoon sugar
10 sweet basil leaves, for garnishing

Heat the oil in a wok, add the onions, and cook until soft. Add the curry paste and stir well. Add the seafood and cook over a high heat for 3–5 minutes.

Stir in the tomato, basil, fish sauce, and sugar, and stir-fry for another 3 minutes. Ladle into a serving dish, garnish with the basil leaves, and serve.

Stir-fried Shrimp Curry
PAD PET KUNG

Shrimp is one of the best kinds of seafood to cook very quickly and they go with all kinds of sauce and dressings.

2 tablespoons oil
1 medium onion, finely sliced
1 tablespoon Home-style Curry Paste
   (see page 31)
1 tablespoon tamarind water (see page 83)
1 tablespoon sugar
1 pound raw jumbo shrimp, peeled and deveined
2 tablespoons fish sauce
3–4 tablespoons water
20 sweet basil leaves

Heat the oil in a frying pan and fry the onion until golden brown. Add the curry paste, tamarind water, and sugar, and stir well.

Add the shrimp, fish sauce, and water, and stir-fry until the shrimp turns a bright orange color. Add the basil and stir-fry over a high heat for a few minutes, then serve.

Steamed Shrimp Curry in Banana Leaf
HAW MOK KUNG

For this recipe, the traditional way to cook and present the curry is in a banana leaf cup. To make each cup, cut two 6-inch circles from a banana leaf, place one on top of the other and fold round into a cup with 1½-inch-high sides. Secure the corners with a staple or a wooden toothpick. You need to make 4 cups for this amount of curry.

14 ounces raw shrimp, peeled, deveined and finely chopped
1 tablespoon Red Curry Paste (see page 28)
1 cup coconut cream (see page 25)
1 teaspoon salt
1 teaspoon sugar
1 tablespoon ground roasted peanuts
40 sweet basil leaves
1 large fresh red chile, finely sliced

2 large banana leaves
Toothpicks

Place the shrimp, curry paste, coconut cream, salt, sugar, and peanuts in a bowl and mix well. Cover and set aside in the fridge for 1 hour.

Place 10 basil leaves in the bottom of each banana-leaf cup. Fill each one with the cold mixture and transfer the cups to a steamer set over boiling water. Steam for 10 minutes. Remove from the steamer, garnish with chile, and serve.

right
Steamed Prawn Curry in Banana Leaf

Shrimp Curry
PENANG KUNG

Another dish that is very popular in my restaurant in Miami. It used to be a special but people kept asking for it so now it's on the menu every day!

2 cups coconut cream (see page 25)
1 tablespoon Penang Curry Paste (see page 29)
2 large handfuls snow peas, cut into 2-inch pieces
2 tablespoons fish sauce
1 tablespoon palm sugar (or soft brown sugar)
1 pound raw shrimp, peeled and deveined, tails on
5 fresh kaffir lime leaves, finely sliced
1 large fresh red chile, finely sliced

Gently heat the coconut cream in a wok, add the curry paste, and stir well. Add the snow peas, fish sauce, and palm sugar, and stir again.

Add the shrimp and simmer for 5 minutes. Stir in the kaffir lime leaves. Spoon into a serving dish, garnish with the chile, and serve.

Spicy Shrimp with Peppercorns
PAD CHA KUNG

This is on my new menu in Ko Samui. Peppercorns are one of the ingredients I grow in my kitchen garden there. Fresh peppercorns are more expensive in the West, where you won't find this kind of dish on the menu so often.

left
Spicy Shrimp with
Peppercorns

3 tablespoons oil
1 tablespoon Kua Curry Paste (see page 30)
2 pounds raw jumbo shrimp, peeled and deveined
3 tablespoons fish sauce
1 teaspoon sugar
1 tablespoon finely sliced *krachai* (see page 23)
4½ tablespoons fresh green peppercorns

Heat the oil in a wok, add the curry paste, stir well, then add the remaining ingredients one at a time, stirring quickly. Cook over a high heat for 2 minutes, then ladle into a dish and serve.

Squid Curry
KARI PLA MUK

If you can find it, fresh squid cooks more quickly and has a less rubbery texture.

2 tablespoons oil
3 tablespoons finely sliced shallots
2 tablespoons finely sliced garlic
2 tablespoons Curry Powder (see page 32)
2 pounds small squid, cleaned and thinly sliced
1 cup coconut cream (see page 25)
5 zucchinis, cut in half lengthways
2 teaspoons salt
2 tablespoons tamarind water (see page 83)
2 teaspoons sugar
1 cup water
2 tomatoes, quartered
1 tablespoon chopped fresh cilantro, for garnishing

Heat the oil in a wok, add the shallots and garlic, and cook until crispy and golden brown. Remove and set aside. Add the curry powder, stir well, then add the squid and stir-fry for 1 minute.

Reduce the heat and stir in the coconut cream, then add the zucchini, salt, tamarind water, sugar, and water. Cook, stirring constantly, for 2 minutes. Add the tomatoes, let it heat through briefly, then garnish with the crispy shallots and garlic, sprinkle with chopped cilantro, and serve.

Pineapple Curry with Mussels
GAENG KUA HOY

How lucky we are in Thailand to have a ready supply of seafood as well as fruit and vegetables. I love this combination of mussels and pineapple. If mussels are not available, use clams.

2 pounds fresh mussels
2 cups coconut cream (see page 25)
2 tablespoons Orange Curry Paste (see page 31)
1 cup water
2 tablespoons fish sauce
1 tablespoon palm sugar (or soft brown sugar)
1 tablespoon tamarind water (see page 83)
14 ounces prepared pineapple, cut into
  small cubes
20 sweet basil leaves

Discard any open or broken mussels, scrub the shells with a brush, and remove any beards. Soak the mussels in cold water for 15 minutes, then drain.

Heat the coconut cream in a large pan, add the curry paste, and stir over a medium heat for 2 minutes. Slowly add the water, bring to a boil, then stir in the fish sauce, palm sugar, and tamarind water. Add the mussels and pineapple and simmer for about 2 minutes. Add the basil and mix well before serving.

Spicy Squid
PAD PET PLA MUK

Serve with rice and wedges of lime to make a main course.

left
Spicy Squid

1½ pounds squid, cut into large pieces and
  scored in a criss-cross fashion with the tip of
  a knife
2 tablespoons lime juice
2 tablespoons oil
1 tablespoon Red Curry Paste (see page 28)
2 tablespoons fish sauce
2 teaspoons sugar
1 medium onion, finely sliced
2 large fresh red chiles, finely sliced
20 sweet basil leaves

Place the squid in a bowl with the lime juice. Cover and let it marinate for 1 hour in the fridge. Heat the oil in a wok, add the curry paste, and stir well. Add the squid and cook over a medium heat for 2 minutes, then add the fish sauce, sugar, onion, chiles, and basil. Stir well for 2 minutes, add the basil leaves and serve.

Squid Curry with Salted Eggs
KARI PLA MUK KAI KEM

I got this recipe from a restaurant in Surat Thani. Usually salted eggs are boiled or fried before use, but here they are marinated and quickly stir-fried, making this quite an unusual dish.

1 pound squid, cleaned and cut into
  2-inch pieces
2 Salted Eggs (see page 34)
1 teaspoon ground turmeric
3 tablespoons oil
2 tablespoons Curry Powder (see page 32)
1 tablespoon tamarind water (see page 83)
1 teaspoon sugar
4 tablespoons water
4 scallions, chopped into 1¼-inch lengths
5 small tomatoes, quartered
10 cilantro stems, roughly chopped
3 tablespoons crispy sliced shallots
2 tablespoons crispy sliced garlic

Place the squid, eggs, and turmeric in a non-metallic bowl, mix together, and let them marinate for 30 minutes in the fridge.

Heat the oil in a wok, stir in the curry powder and marinated squid and eggs, and cook for 1 minute. Add the remaining ingredients one at a time, stirring constantly. The crispy shallots and garlic should be added at the last minute, just before serving.

Crab with Curry Powder
BOO PAD PONG KARI

2 pounds fresh whole crab (uncooked)
2 tablespoons oil
3 garlic cloves, crushed
2 tablespoons Curry Powder (see page 32)
2 eggs
4 whole scallions, cut into 2-inch pieces
1 tablespoon finely chopped ginger
2 tablespoons fish sauce
1 tablespoon light soy sauce
1 teaspoon sugar
2 large fresh red chiles, thinly sliced
Cilantro leaves, for garnishing

Scrub the crab well. Pull back the apron from the underbelly and snap off. Twist off the legs and claws. Pull the body apart and remove the feathery gills and internal organs. Use a cleaver to chop the body into 4 pieces. Crack the claws with a good hit using the back of the cleaver.

Heat the oil in a wok, add the garlic, and fry until golden brown. Add the curry powder and eggs, stir well, then add the crab and stir-fry for 2–3 minutes. Add the scallions, ginger, fish sauce, soy sauce, sugar, and chiles, and cook for 4–5 minutes. Garnish with cilantro and serve.

right
Crab with
Curry Powder

Chili Crab
BOO PAD PET

This dish is a bit tricky to prepare, and like all crab dishes, difficult to eat, but it's worth the effort!

2 x 1-pound fresh whole crabs
(uncooked)
½ cup flour
4 tablespoons oil
1 medium onion, finely chopped
2 tablespoons Penang Curry Paste (see page 29)
1 cup water
2 tablespoons fish sauce
2 teaspoons sugar
2 tablespoons lime juice
4 fresh kaffir lime leaves, finely sliced

Scrub the crabs well. Use a cleaver to chop the crabs in half, then rinse well under cold water, carefully removing the feathery gills and internal organs. Crack the legs and large front claws with a good hit using the back of the cleaver.

Lightly and carefully coat the shells with a little flour. Heat 2 tablespoons of the oil in a large wok and cook the crab, one half at a time, carefully turning the crab in the hot oil until the shell just turns red. Repeat with the remaining crab halves. Remove and drain on paper towels.

Heat the remaining oil in the wok and add the onion and curry paste, stirring well over a medium heat. Add the water, fish sauce, and sugar, and bring to a boil. Return the crab to the wok and simmer for 8–10 minutes. Add the lime juice and lime leaves just before serving.

VEGETABLES AND FRUIT

Vegetables and Fruit
CHAO SUAN

Originally, Thai cooking contained very little meat and was based on fruit and vegetables.
Different parts of Thailand are well known for different fruit and vegetables; Chiang Mai
and the north for lettuce and root vegetables like carrots and potatoes, and Chantaburi
and the southeast for fruits such as rambutan, mangostan, durian, custard apples
(cherimoya), and rose apples. The central plains mainly grow rice, herbs, and spices,
though they are also known for fruits such as mango, pomelo, and papaya. Ko Samui,
where I am now based, is famous for coconuts. The island was very thinly populated

until the arrival of Malay and Chinese fishing families several hundred years ago, some of whom were Muslims who brought their influences into the cuisine. The main industry on the island centered on growing coconuts and shipping them to the mainland to be processed into coconut milk.

Vegetables vary greatly according to the area of the country they are grown in. For example, pineapples tend to be small and dry in the north, big and juicy in Chantaburi, and small and sweet in the south, which is why many restaurants in the south import their pineapples from Chantaburi.

Sweet Potato and Mushroom Curry
GAENG MAN GAP HET

The sweet richness of this red tuber complements the hot and sour flavors of Southeast Asia.

2 cups water
2 tablespoons Jungle Curry Paste (see page 30)
1 pound sweet potato, peeled and cut into
   1-inch cubes
4 ounces oyster mushrooms, washed and
   separated
6 fresh kaffir lime leaves, roughly torn
2 tablespoons light soy sauce
1 teaspoon sugar

Bring the water to a boil in a pan, add the curry paste, and stir well. Add the potato, reduce the heat, and simmer for 10 minutes.

Add the remaining ingredients, cook for another 3 minutes, and serve.

right
Sweet Potato and Mushroom Curry

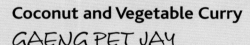

Coconut and Vegetable Curry
GAENG PET JAY

Everyone enjoys this dish, not just vegetarians. To make this an interesting dish, it is important to include a mixture of vegetables with different tastes and textures.

2 tablespoons oil
1 medium onion, roughly chopped
2 tablespoons Massaman Curry Paste
  (see page 29)
2 cups coconut cream (see page 25)
1 teaspoon salt
2 teaspoons sugar
1 pound mixed vegetables (potato, carrot,
  pumpkin), peeled and cut into 1-inch cubes
2 cups water
4 ounces green beans, cut into 1-inch lengths
4 ounces zucchini, cut into 1-inch cubes
2 tablespoons lime juice
2 large fresh green chiles, finely sliced

Heat the oil in a large pan, add the onion and curry paste and stir well. Add the coconut cream, salt, and sugar, bring to a boil, then reduce the heat and simmer for 3 minutes.

Add the potato, carrot, and pumpkin, then cover the pan and cook for 7 minutes, then add the water and bring to a boil, stirring occasionally.

Add the beans and zucchini and cook for a further 5 minutes. Stir in the lime juice and chili and serve immediately.

Southern Vegetable Curry
GAENG LIANG

This curry paste is particular to this dish. It doesn't use many ingredients and is quick to make. White peppercorns have a milder taste than black ones.

left
Southern
Vegetable Curry

4 cups water
4 ounces zucchini, cut into 1-inch cubes
4 ounces pumpkin, cut into 1-inch cubes
4 ounces baby corn cobs (about 10), sliced
  diagonally in half
4 ounces oyster mushrooms, separated
2 medium tomatoes, quartered
20 sweet basil leaves

for the curry paste
1/2 teaspoon white peppercorns
4 small dried red chiles
1/2 teaspoon salt
6 small Thai shallots

First make the curry paste. Pound the peppercorns in a stone mortar to a powder, then add the chiles and pound again. Add the salt and shallots and pound the mixture into a paste.

Bring the water to a boil in a pan and stir in the curry paste. Add the vegetables, reduce the heat, and simmer for 20 minutes, stirring occasionally. Add the basil leaves and serve.

Morning Glory and Mushrooms topped with Curry
PALAM LONGSONG

Morning glory, or water spinach, has long stems and grows in the water. It looks like Western spinach and has a similar taste and texture. Unfortunately morning glory doesn't travel well because the leaves turn yellow quickly and drop off. Thankfully the Chinese love it so much that they now grow and sell it in the West.

1 cup coconut milk
1 tablespoon Penang Curry Paste (see page 29)
2 tablespoons light soy sauce
1 tablespoon tamarind water (see page 83)
1 tablespoon palm sugar (or soft brown sugar)
2 tablespoons ground salted peanuts
1 pound morning glory, chopped into
  2-inch pieces
8 dried Chinese mushrooms, boiled in water
  for 20 minutes, drained and squeezed, stems
  removed, then thinly sliced

Gently heat the coconut milk in a pan, simmer for 5 minutes, stirring. Add the curry paste, stir, then add the soy sauce, tamarind water, and sugar, stirring well. Bring to a boil, stir in the peanuts, cook for 1 minute, then set aside.

Bring a pot of water to a boil, blanch the morning glory until soft, then drain and place on a serving plate. Blanch the mushrooms quickly in the same pot to heat them through and place on top of the morning glory. Pour the curry sauce over them and serve.

Pickled Bamboo Curry
GAENG SOM NORMAI

Pickled bamboo is available in jars from Oriental stores. The bamboo is boiled and then pickled in vinegar, sugar, and salt, giving it a sour taste. Bamboo grows very quickly in Asia so it is often preserved in this way. As with mushrooms, some varieties are poisonous so check first if you are tempted to try this yourself!

4 cups water
2 tablespoons Orange Curry Paste (see page 31)
2 pounds pickled bamboo shoots, thinly sliced
2 large fresh red chiles, finely sliced

Bring the water to a boil in a pan and stir in the curry paste. Reduce the heat, add the bamboo shoots, and simmer for 20 minutes. Add the chiles, and serve.

Vegetarian Samosa in Crispy Tofu Cups
TAO HOU SAMOSA

The filling for this recipe makes enough to make about 30 cups, but you can store it in the fridge for up to 2 days if you don't need that quantity.

Oil, for deep-frying
8 ounces soft tofu, cut into 2-inch squares

for the filling
3 tablespoons oil
2 garlic cloves, finely chopped
1 medium potato, finely chopped
1 medium onion, finely chopped
1 medium carrot, finely chopped
Kernels from 1 ear of corn
2 scallions, finely chopped
1 tablespoon Curry Powder (see page 32)
1/2 teaspoon salt
1 teaspoon sugar
1/2 teaspoon ground black pepper

First make the filling. Heat the oil in a pan and fry the garlic until golden brown. Add the remaining ingredients one at a time, stirring constantly, then cook for 5 minutes. Set aside.

Heat the oil in a wok and deep-fry the tofu until golden brown. Remove and drain on paper towels. Cut a little cross shape in the center of each square and gently scoop a round dent into the piece to make a cup. Place a teaspoon of the filling inside, then serve.

Stir-fried Spicy Mixed Vegetables
GAENG BHAN PAK

2 tablespoons oil
2 garlic cloves, finely chopped
1 tablespoon Home-style Curry Paste
  (see page 31)
1 medium carrot, finely sliced
4 ounces snow peas, trimmed
4 ounces small straw mushrooms, cut in half
  lengthways (a heaped cup)
4 ounces eggplant, cut into 1¼-inch cubes
2 tablespoons light soy sauce
1 teaspoon sugar
20 sweet basil leaves

Heat the oil in a wok and fry the garlic until golden brown. Stir in the curry paste, then add the remaining ingredients. Stir-fry for 3–4 minutes, spoon into a dish, and serve.

Papaya Curry
GAENG LUANG

This is a very hot curry from southern Thailand that is given its bright yellow color by the fresh turmeric. Local people add yellow chiles to the sauce for extra heat and color. It's usually made with shrimp but this is my vegetarian version.

4 cups water
2 pounds green papaya, peeled, seeded and cut into 1¼-inch slices
1 tablespoon tamarind water (see page 83)
4 medium tomatoes, quartered
1 teaspoon salt

for the yellow curry paste
4 small dried red chiles
½ teaspoon salt
1 tablespoon finely chopped lemongrass
1 tablespoon finely chopped garlic
2 teaspoons finely chopped fresh turmeric

First make the curry paste. Pound the chiles in a stone mortar, then add the remaining ingredients one at a time, pounding after each addition, until the mixture forms a paste.

Bring the water to a boil in a pan and stir in the curry paste. Add the papaya, tamarind water, tomatoes, and salt, and simmer for 20 minutes or until the papaya is soft, then serve.

UNRIPE PAPAYAS
Unripe papayas are treated like vegetables in Thailand. They have green skin and flesh and are used in hot dishes and salads, whereas ripe papayas have orange flesh and are eaten as fruit.

Stir-fried Spicy Cauliflower and Long Beans
PAD PET DOK GALAM

We Thais don't like our vegetables to be too soft. They should be quickly stir-fried to keep the texture crunchy. The cauliflower in particular should not be overcooked.

2 tablespoons oil
3 garlic cloves, finely chopped
1 tablespoon Red Curry Paste (see page 28)
1 pound cauliflower, cut into florets
½ cup water
8 ounces long beans, cut into 1¼-inch lengths
2 tablespoons light soy sauce
1 teaspoon sugar
2 tablespoons lime juice

Heat the oil in a wok and fry the garlic until crispy, then remove and set aside. Stir the curry paste into the oil, then add the cauliflower and water and simmer for 3 minutes.

Add the beans, soy sauce, and sugar, and stir-fry for 2 minutes, stirring constantly. Stir in the lime juice, then transfer to a dish. Garnish with the crispy garlic and serve.

LONG BEANS
At up to a yard in length, the aptly named long bean resembles a wildly overgrown string bean (which can be used as a substitute). The long bean, however, is crunchier and cooks faster. Choose darker beans with small seeds inside the pods.

Vegetable Curry
GAENG PET PAK

This is very popular with vegetarians because of the mixture of tastes and textures.

left
Vegetable Curry

2 tablespoons oil
2 tablespoons Red Curry Paste (see page 28)
2 cups coconut cream (see page 25)
2 cups vegetable stock
6 long beans, cut into 1-inch pieces
6 baby corn, cut into 1-inch pieces
6 round Thai eggplants, quartered
1 large carrot, cut into matchsticks
2 large fresh red or green chiles, sliced
4 fresh kaffir lime leaves, roughly chopped
2 teaspoons salt
2 teaspoons sugar
2 tablespoons light soy sauce
30 sweet basil leaves

Heat the oil in a pan and stir in the curry paste. Add the coconut cream, mixing well, then stir in the stock. Add all the vegetables, the lime leaves, salt, sugar, and soy sauce. Stir well, then cook briefly until the vegetables are cooked to your taste. Ladle into a bowl, stir in the basil leaves, and serve.

Stir-fried Spicy Baby Corn and Mushrooms
PAD KIMOW JAY

Baby corn has a wonderfully sweet fragrance and flavor and an irresistible texture. These tiny ears of corn are available both fresh and canned.

3 tablespoons oil
1 tablespoon Home-style Curry Paste
**   (see page 31)**
8 ounces baby corn, thickly sliced
6 ounces oyster mushrooms, separated
2 stems of fresh green peppercorns
2 medium tomatoes, quartered
4 fresh kaffir lime leaves, finely sliced
2 tablespoons light soy sauce
1 teaspoon sugar
2 tablespoons water
1 large fresh red chile, thinly sliced

Heat the oil in a wok, stir in the curry paste, then add the remaining ingredients one at a time, stirring constantly. Cook for 2 minutes, then transfer to a dish and serve.

Stuffed Omelette
MATABAK

This dish was originally a southern Thai Muslim specialty.

3 eggs
1 tablespoon light soy sauce
2 tablespoons oil

for the filling
2 tablespoons oil
2 teaspoons finely chopped garlic
a heaping 1/3 cup finely chopped onions
a heaping 1/3 cup fresh or frozen peas
1/3 cup finely chopped tomatoes
a heaping 1/3 cup finely chopped carrots
1/3 cup finely chopped straw mushrooms
2/3 cup finely chopped peppers
2 teaspoons Curry Powder (see page 32)
2 tablespoons light soy sauce
1/2 teaspoon sugar
1/2 teaspoon ground black pepper

First make the filling. Heat the oil in a pan and fry the garlic until golden. Add the remaining ingredients in the order listed, cooking for about 5–10 minutes and stirring constantly. Remove from the heat and set aside.

Beat the eggs, add the soy sauce, and mix well. Heat the oil in a wok, tilting it to coat the entire surface with the oil.

Pour in the egg and tip the wok to spread evenly. When the egg has dried, pour the filling into the center. Fold in the sides of the omelette to make a square package. Cook briefly to warm through the filling, then lift carefully onto a dish and serve.

right
Stuffed Omelette

Vegetable Curry with Pickled Garlic
GAENG PAK KRATIAM DONG

Pickled garlic is a powerful flavoring—whole heads of garlic are preserved in a rich, salty liquid (see page 98).

3 tablespoons oil
2 tablespoons Curry Powder (see page 32)
2 whole heads of Pickled Garlic, sliced (see page 34)
4 tablespoons water
6 ounces mixed vegetables (carrots, beans, corn, celery), cut into small pieces
2 scallions, cut into 1¼-inch lengths
1/2 teaspoon salt
1 tablespoon chopped fresh cilantro

Heat the oil in a wok, stir in the curry powder, then add the remaining ingredients in the order listed, stirring constantly. Cook for 2–3 minutes, then transfer to a dish and serve, garnished with the cilantro.

Pineapple Curry

GAENG KUA SAPPAROT

If you buy a pineapple and find it is too sour to eat on its own, this is a great way to use it and bring out the flavor.

left
Pineapple Curry

2 tablespoons oil
2 tablespoons Kua Curry Paste (see page 30)
2 cups coconut cream (see page 25)
1 cup water
2 tablespoons light soy sauce
1/2 teaspoon salt
2 tablespoons lime juice
4 fresh kaffir lime leaves, thinly sliced
1 fresh pineapple, trimmed and cut into small cubes
Finely chopped red chile, for the garnish

Heat the oil in a pan and fry the curry paste, stirring well. Stir in the coconut cream. Add the water, slowly bring to a boil, then add the soy sauce, salt, lime juice, lime leaves, and pineapple. Simmer for 3 minutes, then transfer to a bowl, garnish with chile, and serve.

Spicy Mushroom Curry

HET PAD PET

This is a great dish for vegetarians because mushrooms have a meaty, satisfying texture. Use a mixture such as chestnut, oyster, and other wild mushrooms.

1 cup coconut cream (see page 25)
1 pound mixed mushrooms, chopped
1 tablespoon Orange Curry Paste (see page 31)
2 tablespoons light soy sauce
1 teaspoon sugar
1 tablespoon finely sliced *krachai* (see page 23)
1 large fresh red chile, finely sliced
20 basil leaves

Gently heat the coconut cream in a pan, stirring well for 2 minutes. Add the mushrooms, cook for 2 minutes, then stir in the remaining ingredients in the order listed, and cook for another 2 minutes. Transfer to a dish and serve.

Stir-fried Eggplants with Green Curry Paste and Bean Sauce
MAKUA PAT KEOW WAN

This curry can be made with any eggplants, the common large purple ones as seen on the right or small round Thai eggplants as below. If the purple ones are used they should be cooked until soft, whereas the tiny Thai eggplants are better left al dente.

2 tablespoons oil
2 tablespoons Green Curry Paste (see page 28)
1 pound eggplants, cut into 1-inch cubes
4 tablespoons vegetable stock or water
1 cup red pepper, cored, seeded, and cut
  lengthways into thin strips
1 tablespoon bean sauce
1 tablespoon light soy sauce
1 tablespoon sugar
2 large fresh red chiles, thinly sliced
20 holy basil leaves

Heat the oil in a pan and stir in the curry paste. Stir in the eggplant and stock, and cook until the eggplant begins to soften (about 5 minutes). Add the remaining ingredients, stirring constantly. Cook for 1 minute and serve.

EGGPLANTS
The purple-black eggplant common in the West is used in Thai cooking, along with several other varieties less familiar to Westerners. The Thai eggplants most commonly available in Oriental supermarkets is round, pale green and about an inch in diameter (as seen left). The smaller Thai pea eggplant is generally rarer outside Thailand and tastes more bitter (see picture on page 12).

Chickpea Curry

GAENG PET TUA

Chickpeas are not commonly used in Thai cooking—this dish shows its Indian roots.

2 tablespoons oil
2 tablespoons Massaman Curry Paste
(see page 29)
2 cups coconut cream (see page 25)
2 cups water
2 medium potatoes, peeled and cut into
1-inch cubes
1^1/$_3$ cups dried chickpeas, soaked overnight,
or use canned
2 small onions, cut into 1-inch squares
2 large fresh red chiles, cut lengthways into
thin slivers
2 tablespoons light soy sauce
^{1}/$_2$ teaspoon salt
1 tablespoon sugar

Heat the oil in a pan and stir in the curry paste. Stir in the coconut cream, mixing well, then add the remaining ingredients in the order given.

Bring to a boil and simmer for about 15 minutes until the potatoes and chickpeas are cooked. Transfer to a dish and serve.

Tofu and Ginger Curry

KARI TAO HOU

Tofu is an ingredient that came to Thailand with the Chinese. Putting tofu into an Indian-style curry is a good example of how Thai food has fused elements of Chinese and Indian cooking.

Oil, for deep-frying
1 pound tofu, cut into 1-inch cubes
2 tablespoons oil
2 tablespoons Curry Powder (see page 32)
1 cup coconut cream (see page 25)
2 tablespoons light soy sauce
1 tablespoon tamarind water (see page 83)
1 teaspoon sugar
3 tablespoons water
1 tablespoon finely sliced ginger

Heat the oil in a wok and deep-fry the tofu until golden brown on all sides. Drain on kitchen paper and set aside.

Heat the 2 tablespoons of oil in a second wok and stir in the curry powder. Add the remaining ingredients in the order given, stirring constantly, and cook for 2 minutes. Stir in the fried tofu, cook for another 2 minutes, then serve.

Green Curry with Young Coconut
GAENG KEOW WAN MAPROW

You can find young green coconuts (see below) in Oriental stores and they are also available canned. You need two young green coconuts for this recipe. Cut them open, drain off the coconut water (a refreshing drink when chilled), and use the coconut flesh. Traditionally this curry is served inside the coconut shell.

2 tablespoons oil
2 garlic cloves, finely chopped
2 tablespoons Green Curry Paste (see page 28)
2 cups coconut cream (see page 25)
2 cups water
6 ounces young coconut flesh, thinly sliced
(see above)
2 large fresh red chiles, sliced diagonally into
thin ovals
1 teaspoon salt
8 round Thai eggplants, quartered
2 teaspoons sugar
20 sweet basil leaves

Heat the oil in a large pan, add the garlic, and fry until golden brown. Stir in the curry paste, mixing well. Add the coconut cream and keep stirring for 2 minutes.

Slowly add the water and bring to a boil, stirring constantly. Add the sliced coconut, chiles, salt, eggplants, and sugar. Simmer for about 3 minutes until the eggplants are cooked. Stir in the basil leaves just before pouring into a bowl and serve.

Boiled Egg Curry
GAENG KAI

Makes a good breakfast or lunch dish.

2 tablespoons oil
5 small shallots, finely sliced
3 garlic cloves, finely sliced
2 tablespoons Massaman Curry Paste
  (see page 29)
½ cup water
3 cardamom pods
5 whole cloves
2-inch piece of cinnamon stick
½ cup coconut milk
2 teaspoons salt
1 tablespoon palm sugar (or soft brown sugar)
6 hard-boiled eggs, peeled and cut in half
2 large fresh red chiles, sliced

for the garnish
1 tablespoon deep-fried onions
2 large fresh red chiles, finely sliced
Cilantro leaves

Heat the oil in a pan and fry the shallots and garlic for 2 minutes. Stir in the curry paste, mixing well. Add the water and the remaining ingredients in the order given. Simmer gently for 10 minutes. Garnish with the deep-fried onions, chiles, and cilantro leaves, and serve.

Conversion Table

Weight (solids)

7g	1/4 oz.
10g	1/3 oz.
15g	1/2 oz.
20g	3/4 oz.
30g	1 oz.
40g	1 1/2 oz.
55g	2 oz.
70g	2 1/2 oz.
85g	3 oz.
100g	3 1/2 oz.
115g	4 oz. (1/4 lb.)
125g	4 1/2 oz.
155g	5 1/2 oz.
170g	6 oz.
200g	7 oz.
225g	8 oz. (1/2 lb.)
255g	9 oz.
285g	10 oz.
300g	10 1/2 oz.
310g	11 oz.
325g	11 1/2 oz.
340g	12 oz. (3/4 lb.)
370g	13 oz.
400g	14 oz.
425g	15 oz.
450g	1 lb.
510g	18 oz.
570g	1 1/4 lb.
680g	1 1/2 lb.
790g	1 3/4 lb.
900g	2 lb.
1kg	35 oz.
1.1kg	2 1/2 lb.
1.2kg	2 3/4 lb.
1.4kg	3 lb.
1.5kg	3 1/4 lb.
1.6kg	3 1/2 lb.
1.8kg	4 lb.
2kg	4 1/2 lb.
2.3kg	5 lb.
2.5kg	5 1/2 lb.
3.1kg	6 3/4 lb.

Volume (liquids)

5ml	1 teaspoon
15ml	1 tablespoon or 1/2fl. oz.
30ml	1fl. oz.
45ml	1 1/2fl. oz.
60ml	2fl. oz. (1/4 cup)
90ml	3fl. oz. (1/3 cup)
100ml	3 1/2fl. oz.
120ml	4fl. oz. (1/2 cup)
150ml	5fl. oz. (2/3 cup)
180ml	6fl. oz. (3/4 cup)
210ml	7fl. oz.
240ml	8fl. oz. (1 cup)
270ml	9fl. oz.
300ml	10fl. oz. (1 1/4 cups)
330ml	11fl. oz.
360ml	12fl. oz. (1 1/2 cups)
380ml	13fl. oz.
410ml	14fl. oz. (1 3/4 cups)
440ml	15fl. oz.
480ml	16fl. oz. (2 cups)
500ml (0.5 liter)	17fl. oz.
540ml	18fl. oz. (2 1/4 cups)
600ml	20fl. oz.
650ml	22fl. oz. (2 3/4 cups)
700ml	24fl. oz. (3 cups)
820ml	28fl. oz. (3 1/2 cups)
950ml	32fl. oz. (4 cups)
1 liter	33.8fl. oz.
1.2 liters	40fl. oz. (5 cups)
1.4 liters	48fl. oz. (6 cups)
1.8 liters	60fl. oz. (7 1/2 cups)
2 liters	68fl. oz. (8 1/2 cups)

Length

6mm	1/4 inch
1cm	3/8 inch
2cm	3/4 inch
2.5cm	1 inch
3cm	1 1/4 inches
4cm	1 1/2 inches
5cm	2 inches
7.5cm	3 inches
10cm	4 inches
15cm	6 inches
18cm	7 inches
20.5cm	8 inches
25.5cm	10 inches
28cm	11 inches
30.5cm	12 inches

Oven temperatures

CELSIUS*	FAHRENHEIT	GAS	DESCRIPTION
110 C	225 F	mark 1/4	cool
130 C	250 F	mark 1/2	cool
140 C	275 F	mark 1	very low
150 C	300 F	mark 2	very low
170 C	325 F	mark 3	low
180 C	350 F	mark 4	moderate
190 C	375 F	mark 5	mod. hot
200 C	400 F	mark 6	hot
220 C	425 F	mark 7	hot
230 C	450 F	mark 8	very hot

*For fan-assisted ovens, reduce temperatures by 10°C

Index